Preface

Britain's inland waterways are a vital part ᵒ they have shaped our landscapes, communities and economic life. Today, as a focus for regeneration, they once again bring major benefits to the communities they connect.

Last year witnessed the opening of the Millennium Ribble Link, connecting the Lancaster Canal to the rest of the inland waterways network and allowing boats to cruise from London to Lancaster for the first time ever.

With plans to restore the Lancaster Canal north to Kendal advancing at a rapid pace, boaters will one day be able to travel from southern England to the Lake District, bringing increased tourism, new jobs and an enhanced environment to millions more in the north west of England.

So much of what has been achieved to date is the result of partnership. It is about the public, private, community and voluntary sector coming together. It is about the Lancaster Canal Trust, British Waterways, The Waterways Trust and so many others working together to provide the Lancaster Canal with a new lease of life.

We congratulate the Lancaster Canal Trust for all their hard work and commitment to the canal and the restoration of the Northern Reaches.

Roger Hanbury
Chief Executive
The Waterways Trust
MARCH 2003

Cruise the Lancaster Canal with A.C.E.
•

If you are a confirmed Cruiser and would like to join us please contact the Membership Secretary:

Mrs Doreen Hood
8 Marsh Lane Cottages, Cockerham LA2 0EJ
Tel: 01524 792081 Mobile: 07971 876247

The Complete Guide to the Lancaster Canal

INTRODUCTION

This guide covers the Lancaster Canal from the confluence of the Ribble Link with the River Ribble at Preston to Kendal and the branch to Glasson. It includes everything that the visitor to the canal needs to know to make the best use of their time.

Maps are drawn to a scale of 1:25000 and are based on the Ordnance Survey Map, reproduced with the permission of the Controller of Her Majesty's Stationery Office, Crown copyright reserved.

The authors wish to acknowledge the contribution made by Nik Bruce of the Lancashire Trust for Nature Conservation and British Waterways Board.

Every effort has been made to ensure this guide is accurate and up to date, but errors inevitably occur. In order to help future revisions the Lancaster Canal Trust would be pleased to hear of any mistakes or omissions you may notice. Write to:

> David Slater
> 91 Cop Lane
> Penwortham
> Preston
> Lancs PR1 9AH

First edition published in 1989 by The Lancaster Canal Trust; revised 2000.
Third edition published in 2003 by The Lancaster Canal Trust.
The Lancaster Canal trust is a Registered Charity No. 240957

Authors: David Slater, Martin Main, Jon Clark and Lesley Blundell.
Photography: Graham C. Agnew, Reg Phillips and David Slater
Designed by Graham C. Agnew; Printed by HSP Milners, Barrow-in-Furness
ISBN 0-9514146-2-3

FOREWORD

Lancashire and Cumbria are counties of contrast! To the south lie the great conurbations of Manchester and Liverpool; to the north the Lake District, the Howgills and the mass of high ground that separates England and Scotland whilst the area around Arnside and Silverdale offers some of the finest countryside anywhere, yet an area which the motorist speeding up the M6, anxious to get to the Lakes, tends to ignore. To the west, where Lancashire meets the Irish Sea lie the resorts of Blackpool, Morecambe, Lytham and St. Annes and Fleetwood. To the east, the Pennines form a natural boundary, the rolling heather clad hills of Bleasdale and Quernmore offering easy walking, but with fine views across the Fylde plain to the sea, whilst the valleys of the Lune, Wyre and Ribble contain picturesque villages and winding lanes.

Both counties are rich in history! Vikings, Romans, all have left their mark on the landscape. The castles at Lancaster, Clitheroe and Kendal bear witness to the more troubled times of the past. But perhaps the most important time in Lancashire's history was the Industrial Revolution! The canal age began with the Bridgewater Canal just outside Manchester whilst the sons of Lancashire pioneered many inventions that were to make the county one of the most important industrial areas in the country, founded on cotton. Unfortunately, cotton is no longer king, but the decline of the industry has enabled the county to cast off its image of 'dark satanic mills', although its past importance is remembered in several museums devoted to this aspect of Lancashire life. Cumbria never achieved the industrial status of its southern cousin, but utilised its natural assets – gunpowder manufacture being an important industry in the villages south of Kendal, whilst quarrying limestone and slate is still an important feature of the local economy.

Lancashire, north of Preston, and South Cumbria is very much farming country and the towns and villages have changed little over the years. Lancaster owes its origins to its status as the main port on the west coast before the development of Liverpool, leaving a legacy of many fine buildings and past industries based on Lancaster's important trade with the African colonies and the New World. Gillow the furniture manufacturer, famous the world over, founded his business in Lancaster using the tropical hardwoods that were being imported through the port. Through it all runs the Lancaster Canal, built to transport coal north and limestone south, almost bisecting the area and making it an ideal base for those wishing to explore the riches of this part of the world. Frequent bus services make travelling easy for the visitor. The main railway line from London to Scotland passes through Preston and Lancaster making for easy access to the canal. From Preston, Lancaster and Carnforth lines radiate to the cities of Liverpool, Manchester and Leeds, to the Yorkshire Dales and to Blackpool. From Carnforth the West Cumbria line is a delight, hugging the northern shore of Morecambe Bay whilst a branch line from Oxenholme reaches right into the Lake District at Windermere.

Whether you come for a day, a week or a month, South Cumbria and North Lancashire has so much to offer with the Lancaster Canal providing the ideal base from which to visit the area. It is not possible to include in this guide everything there is to see and do along the canal, but it is intended to provide a flavour of what is there so that, the visitor will be able to plan his or her visit, whatever its length.

A HISTORY OF THE LANCASTER CANAL

In the middle of the Eighteenth Century, Lancaster was a prosperous town and port. Ideally situated on the west coast, it was the main route between the old and the new worlds. Manufactured goods from the industries of Yorkshire left the country through Lancaster for the developing Americas and returning ships brought in the produce of this rich new territory, which formed the basis for much of Lancaster's industry and prosperity, whilst a few miles to the north at Kendal, snuff and tobacco curing established itself. But there were ominous signs on the horizon! As ships grew in size, so did the difficulties of navigating the notorious estuary of the River Lune, thus threatening the prosperity of Lancaster and the smaller port of Milnthorpe, whilst to the south Liverpool was growing in importance.

In an effort to save Lancaster, the merchants proposed building a canal, which, starting at Kendal and running almost due south through Lancaster, would reach Preston from where it would run south-westwards, passing through Leyland to the village of Parbold to join the Leeds & Liverpool Canal, thus providing a direct link between Lancaster and the port of Liverpool. The famous canal engineer James Brindley, responsible for the construction of much of England's canal network, was asked to make a survey, though it is more likely that Robert Whitworth, his pupil, undertook the work.

The scheme did not attract much support in the town. An alternative idea of building a new port at Glasson at the mouth of the Lune found favour; the idea of a canal was dropped. However, there was a still a group who extolled the virtues of having Lancaster on the canal map and in the 1770's, John Rennie was asked to re-survey the canal. Rennie's proposal followed much of Whitworth's original route to Preston, but here Rennie's line crossed the Ribble then struck out south-eastwards towards Chorley, thence east of Wigan to Westhoughton, for Rennie was basing his canal, not on trade with America, but on coal from the South Lancashire coalfield and limestone from quarries around Kendal and Milnthorpe. Rennie knew from what had happened on the Bridgewater Canal just how valuable a cargo of coal could be, fuelling industry and home alike, but how difficult its carriage on land could be. Limestone was important not only for building purposes, but also as a soil conditioner and would be in demand in the agricultural belt of West Lancashire. That Rennie proposed that the canal should be capable of taking broad beam craft, up to seventy two feet in length, is an indication that he had designs on linking the canal to the Bridgewater Canal, and thus the main canal system. In the event this did not happen.

Rennie's proposals found favour throughout Lancashire and south Westmorland as Cumbria was then known. An Act of Parliament was obtained, construction beginning in 1792. The company was dogged by financial problems from the start, and by the end of the century only the section from Walton Summit, five miles south of Preston to Wigan, and the section northwards from Preston to Tewitfield, had been completed, the two sections being linked with a temporary tramway. However, by 1826 the canal was through to Kendal and a branch to Glasson Dock had been built. The northern and southern sections were never linked by water, the tramway becoming permanent. This so-called 'southern section' is now part of the Leeds–Liverpool canal from Johnson's Hillock to Wigan, and retains many of Rennie's features, but is not included in this guide. Rennie designed 22 aqueducts on the full line of the Lancaster Canal, several have been destroyed or replaced but, of the remainder, those over the Wyre (bridge 61), Conder (87), Lune (107), Keer (132) and at Sedgwick (178) are especially notable.

Eventually the southern section was leased, then sold, to the Leeds and Liverpool Canal and all hope of the Canal ever being linked to the main network disappeared. Despite this, the canal flourished, carrying not only coal and limestone, but all manner of goods, until the coming of the railways.

At first the railways did not pose a threat, for by the mid Nineteenth Century the spread of metals from the Midlands had only reached Preston. The canal company had introduced passenger carrying boats and these provided the most comfortable means of transport then available for travellers in North Lancashire, the 'packet' boats completing the trip from Kendal to Preston (and vice versa) in around eight hours. Even the building of the Lancaster and Preston Railway did not pose a threat; upon its opening the canal company immediately halved its tolls on goods carried on the canal and withdrew the packet boat service south of Lancaster. The effect was to force the railway to rely on a small amount of passenger traffic, something it could not afford to do, and this set the scene for something almost unique in waterways history, that of a canal company taking over a railway, and for a time the railway and canal operated alongside one another. The proposal to build a railway between Carlisle and Lancaster was another matter, since this would take the tracks not only into the area served by the canal, but beyond! The proposal was vigorously opposed by the canal company, but to no avail. Matters were further complicated because the act authorising the railways construction conferred powers to link into the track of the Lancaster and Preston Railway and also to run through trains to Preston and the South. The canal company tried to fight back by providing as much hindrance as possible to through traffic on the railway, but the final nail in the coffin came when an accident occurred at Bay Horse, south of Lancaster, an express from Carlisle running into the rear of a local train from Lancaster, with a resultant loss of life. After this the canal company was instructed not to resist the passage of trains from the Lancaster & Carlisle Railway and the canal became unable to compete. Eventually the canal was leased by the then London & North Western Railway Company and later bought outright, a special medal being struck to commemorate the event. The Lancaster Canal Company had ceased to exist and this chapter in the history of the canal closed.

Despite this the railway continued to operate the canal, finding it to be an excellent supply of water for depots at Preston, Lancaster and Carnforth, but now the railways were facing competition this time from the roads. Canal traffic to Kendal ceased in 1944 and the last traffic carried on the canal was a consignment of coal from Barrow, via Glasson Dock to Storey's at Lancaster. From Kendal to Stainton the canal was progressively dewatered, having suffered great losses of water through seepage into the porous limestone over which the canal is built. In the 1960's, the Ministry of Transport proposed culverting the canal north of Carnforth in six places, thus denying access to this lovely section of canal. Despite vigorous opposition the Ministry's plans went ahead as the M6 motorway was extended northwards, leaving only forty two of the original fifty four miles of canal north of Preston open to traffic.

Following the transfer of ownership to the London & North Western Railway Company, the grouping of railways in 1923 led to a further transfer to the London, Midland & Scottish Railway. With railway nationalisation in 1948, control passed to the British Transport Commission, and subsequently by the 1962 Transport Act to the British Waterways Board, in whose control it is today.

Of the tramway, what remains today is in the control of Preston Borough Council and is a public right of way, providing an interesting route for a walk or cycle, south from Avenham Park, Preston to Bamber Bridge. Further south the site of the transfer basin from the tramway to the Southern Section of the Lancaster Canal is now lost in a housing estate at Clayton Brook, but the line of the canal can be found at Whittle-le-Woods (bridge and tunnel) before the remaindered arm of the Lancaster canal can be seen at its junction with the Leeds and Liverpool Canal at Johnson's Hillock.

CRUISING ON THE LANCASTER CANAL

The main line of the canal offers 41 miles of relaxing, lock free boating and for the more energetic there are the six locks down to Glasson Basin. The absence of locks means that the majority of the canal is available for cruising all year round. Sections are occasionally closed in the Winter as publicised in the British Waterways national stoppage programme. If in doubt you can contact the British Waterways Lancaster Canal Office (tel. 01524 751888 Fax: 01524 751133).

Mooring: In theory you can moor anywhere on the towpath side unless there is specific indication to the contrary. However, in places bankside vegetation can extend several feet into the channel and care must be exercised when mooring away from established sites. The canal was built as a barge waterway – the channel is a shallow 'V' and skippers of narrow boats and other deep drafted craft may find a plank is required for egress and access. Do not moor where your boat is a hazard to navigation such as at bends, junctions or locks. British Waterways provide approved visitor moorings with facilities for rubbish disposal etc. and these should be used where possible. Approach the bank slowly, front first, at a slight angle and allow a member of the crew to step off the boat. Put the engine in neutral and pull the back of the boat in with your rope. The boat must be tied up at the front and back but never tie ropes across the towing path where they could be a hazard to walkers and other users. When leaving, push the boat away from the bank before engaging the engine, to prevent the propeller damaging the bed of the canal or itself. Do not moor longer than necessary at water points or sanitary stations.

On the Move: You should keep to the centre of the channel but move over to the right when meeting oncoming boats and pass left to left. Overtake on the left. On some of the shallower sections it is possible to run aground near the edges. You should be able to simply reverse off but may have to use a boat pole, making sure the crew is well away from where the boat is stuck. The official speed limit is 4 m.p.h., a fast walking pace. However, if your wash breaks on the bank, you are going too fast, using more fuel than you need, and more importantly you will also be causing damage to the canal banks. In shallow water, boats will actually travel faster if you reduce speed, because over-revving pulls the bottom of the boat deeper into the water. Do not overtake on a bend, near a bridge, lock or where you cannot see the way ahead. Slow down when being overtaken so as to have steerage way. Slow down when passing anglers, moored boats, other moving craft or repair works. Please do not disturb the peace of the waterway by playing radios, stereos or televisions too loud.

Locks: If you are hiring a boat for the first time ensure the boatyard gives you adequate instruction but remember the following points. Share locks with boats travelling in the same direction. If there is a boat coming in the opposite direction and the lock is in their favour i.e. you would need to either fill or empty it first, then wait for them to pass through. This saves water and some effort on your part. When leaving a lock always ensure that all the paddles are down and the gates are closed, unless there is a boat approaching from the opposite direction when it is courteous to leave the gates open for them. Obey all instructions for the use of locks provided by British Waterways or its staff.

There are British Waterways sanitary stations at Tewitfield, Carnforth, Lancaster, Galgate, Garstang, Bilsborrow and Cadley to which access is provided by a BW 'smart card' obtainable from the BW Lancaster office at Galgate (Tel: 01524 751888).

Dimensions: For the more statistically minded the maximum dimensions for cruising craft are given below:

Main Line

Maximum length	75 feet/22.86 metres (for turning)
Maximum width	14 feet/4.26 metres
Maximum headroom	6 feet 10 inches/2 metres (Ashton)
	Elsewhere 8 feet/2.4 metres (bridge 129b)
Maximum draught	3 feet/0.9 metres

Glasson Branch

Maximum length	70 feet/21.3 metres
Maximum width	14 feet/4.26 metres
Maximum headroom	8 feet/2.4 metres

Millennium Ribble Link

Maximum length	72 feet/21.9 metres

Width and draught clearances are inter-related, full details are available from British Waterways.

Lancaster Canal Boat Club

Affiliated to JWA & AWCC

For Family Events on the Lancaster Canal

JOIN THE CLUB!

Membership Secretary
Mrs Sandra Henstock
170 Penrose Avenue, Marton
Blackpool FY4 4JX

Tel 01253 764171

FISHING THE LANCASTER CANAL

Angling is permitted from the towing path side on both the cruising and remainder sections between Preston and Stainton. The main fish species are Roach, Perch and Bream, with smaller numbers of Pike, Tench, Ruffe, Crucian Carp, Gudgeon and Chub. Eel occur throughout the canal. The best fishing areas are the rural stretches between Preston and Lancaster, particularly on the Glasson Branch. There is also good fishing on the Northern Reaches above Tewitfield and on the rural stretches north of Carnforth.

Before fishing you will require an Environment Agency rod license. These can be obtained from most of the local tackle shops, the nearest to the canal being in Lancaster, Garstang and Preston. You will also require a British Waterways angling permit, for which there is a charge, obtainable from the Waterway Office, Main Road, Galgate, Lancaster LA2 0LQ (tel: 01524 751888; Fax: 01524 751133). At present angling is not permitted between 15th March to 15th June inclusive but this restriction may be lifted during the currency of this guide. The Lancaster Canal is an important leisure area for boaters and walkers as well as anglers so please observe the following code of conduct:

> *Do not obstruct the towing path.*
>
> *Always take litter home and light no fires.*
>
> *Take care under power lines.*
>
> *When a boat approaches, lift your rod and line to one side.*
>
> *Do not fish at locks, bridge holes or from landing stages.*

Further information may be obtained from local tackle shops or by contacting the British Waterways Lancaster Canal Office.

WALKING THE LANCASTER CANAL

Much of the towpath of the canal is not a public right of way but British Waterways encourage its use and it provides easy walking throughout its entire length in mainly rural surroundings. Access points are numerous and there are many fingerposts and waymark boards to show the way. The towpath from Ashton Basin in Preston to Tewitfield, including the Glasson Branch, is continuous, wide and generally speaking in excellent condition. From Ashton Basin as far as Br. 19 the towpath is surfaced with stone but elsewhere it is generally grassed; - it can be muddy during winter months and after wet weather particularly in Salwick and Ashton cuttings. In Lancaster the towpath is surfaced from Br. 95 to Br. 110 and again in Carnforth from the basin north to Br. 129. Further towpath improvements are in hand.

North of Tewitfield the towpath is a definitive public footpath through to Canal Head in Kendal. Several short diversions are necessary due to road crossings, but these are either obvious or well signposted. The towpath as far as Stainton (the northern limit of the watered section) is in excellent condition, but beyond here the route of the canal is in  various ownerships and is less well maintained. The horse path over Hincaster Hill is listed as an Ancient Monument. North of the tunnel the towpath is missing due to the intrusion of the A.590 and a diversion for about half a mile along Hincaster Lane is needed, but after the crossing of the A.590 the line of the canal can be regained by a short if steep climb up the hillside. From Sedgwick into Kendal much of the channel has been infilled but the line of the former towpath is obvious, the only obstacles being the occasional stile.

The opening of a footpath along much of the line of the Millennium Ribble Link now offers a fine long distance circular walk utilising the Lancashire Coastal Way. This way-marked route follows the shoreline of Lancashire as closely as possible from Southport to the border of Cumbria near Arnside using existing footpaths and other highways. The section along Blackpool Road just west of Preston intersects with the Millennium Ribble Link path. Leaflets describing the route of the Lancashire Coastal Way are available from the County Council Information Centres.

Enjoy walking in safety and observe the following code of conduct:-

Wear stout shoes, boots in winter and take a waterproof.

Keep away from the canal edge and make sure that children are supervised.

Always follow the country code.

Obey British Waterways by-laws and share the towing path with other users.

The canal is covered by Ordnance Survey Landranger maps Nos. 97 and 102. South Lakeland District Council and Lancaster City Council publish a leaflet covering the canal between Lancaster and Kendal. There are several publications covering walks off the canal and the Lancaster Canal Trust has recently researched three circular walks on behalf of Lancashire County Council, and published in leaflet form by the Arnside/Silverdale AONB Countryside Management Service covering the Holme and Tewitfield areas. These can obtained from the County Council Information Centres or from the Arnside/Silverdale Countryside Management Service Office (tel: 01524 761034). Wyre Borough Council publishes a number of leaflets covering walks in and around Garstang (some of which are easily accessible from the canal) which are obtainable from Garstang Tourist Information Centre (tel: 01995 602125).

THE NATURAL HISTORY OF THE CANAL

It would be impossible in such a short article to fully describe all the wildlife which lives along the canal, and the examples given here are only a fraction of what can be seen on a walk along the towpath.

The canal forms a "corridor" for wildlife through towns and areas of intense farming, where otherwise it would be hard-pressed to find places to survive.

The canal is at its most spectacular in summer, when the banks are thick with water-loving wild flowers, such as the sweet-smelling meadow sweet (which was collected in times past to freshen the air in houses) and even relatives of our kitchen herbs: water mint, wild angelica, watercress and marjoram.

The different types of bankings along the canal support different plant communities. The old collapsed earth banks support the widest variety of plants, while those which have recently been rebuilt using steel piles are the poorest. The stone walls of the locks are different again, with ferns, mosses and lichens (which love the damp, shady conditions) growing in the cracks.

Some plants grow in the water itself: on the submerged walls, especially below the numerous old bridges which cross the canal, can be seen bright green mats of a type of fresh water sponge, which sometimes grows out into the water like "fingers"; the tall velvet heads of "reedmace" (also called bulrush by some people) are easily recognised; one of the most common plants is "sweetflag". The leaves of this plant smell very fragrant when crushed and, at first glance, look very similar to flag iris, hence its name; both yellow and white water lily can be found, but yellow is the more common. Most people are familiar with the floating round leaves and flowers of water lily in summer, but the plants can also be seen in winter, especially if the water is clear, growing on the bottom of the canal and looking very much like cabbages.

There are a number of places along the canal which are particularly rich in plants: the length from Salwick to Swillbrook, north of Garstang, near Forton and at Galgate. North of Tewitfield, there is a change in the type of plants present, as the limestone of the Silverdale area begins to influence the soil. Harebells, lady's bedstraw and cut-leaved cranesbill can be found here.

The canal is attractive to a range of birds: yellow hammer and bullfinch flit in the hedges which line much of the towpath. On the canal itself, mute swan, coot, moorhen and mallard can be seen. The swans and mallard are especially common in the built-up areas, attracted by the prospect of an easy meal.

A number of other birds visit the canal to feed. In summer, swallows and martins can be seen flying low over the water surface, catching insects; heron wade in the shallows, stalking sticklebacks and frogs; very occasionally, you may catch sight of the bright blue flash of a kingfisher as it darts swiftly up the canal.

The thick bankside vegetation provides cover for small mammals such as shrews, bank voles and water voles. Even though they themselves are seldom seen, signs of their presence can be found by all those who care to look – small passageways in the grass and the chewed remains of a plant stalk or rosehip.

The summer display of wild flowers attracts a number of butterflies, including meadow brown, tortoiseshell, red admiral and common blue. Dragonflies and the smaller, more colourful damselflies (or "horse-stingers" and "devil's darning needles" as they used to be called) can be seen as they dart "mechanically" about, or bask on the tall bankside plants. As adults, they often survive in the open air for little more than a week or two, after having spent from two to three years living under the water as nymphs. Many other insects are associated with the canal, living in or even on it, like the long-legged pond skater and the small whirly-gig beetle (which seems to spend most of its life madly spinning on the same spot), both of which are supported by the water's surface tension.

From the nature conservation point of view, the Lancaster Canal is very valuable, not only as it acts as "wildlife reservoir" and "corridor" (allowing plants and animals to recolonise the surrounding land), but because it gives the public access to a long stretch of countryside, hopefully not only to bring enjoyment, but also to educate, for, with a better understanding of what is present in our countryside, there must surely come a wider call for its protection.

TRANSPORT

The position of the canal on its north/south axis makes it an ideal base for exploring much of North Lancashire and South Cumbria. The canal is well served by both rail and bus services.

Railways

The London – Glasgow main line runs parallel to the canal for most of its way. There are major stations at Preston, Lancaster, Carnforth and Oxenholme. From Preston, trains are available to Blackpool and the Fylde coast, Blackburn, Clitheroe and Burnley, Manchester and Liverpool. Lancaster is the junction for services to Morecambe. At Carnforth a line goes off to Barrow-in-

Carnforth Station

Furness, through Silverdale, Arnside and Grange-over-Sands, and is well worth a trip for the picturesque countryside of Furness and South Lakeland. This line continues along the west coast of Cumbria, providing access to Sellafield, the Ravenglass & Eskdale Railway, the towns of Whitehaven and Workington and finally Carlisle. Carnforth is also the junction for the line running up Lunesdale through Settle and Skipton to Leeds. Oxenholme junction is the start of the branch to Kendal and Windermere.

Buses

The main operators in the area are Stagecoach Ribble and Stagecoach Cumberland. Other services are operated by the municipal undertakings in the main towns and of course Blackpool has its famous trams which operate along the coast to Fleetwood. In general bus services operate on a similar pattern to the railways with certain exceptions; Blackpool is accessible by bus from Garstang, a service operates up the Lune valley from Lancaster to Kirkby Lonsdale and also Ingleton, famous for its falls. An hourly service operates from Preston direct to the Trafford Centre outside Manchester. In South Cumbria services are more sparse the main route serving the canal being the 555 service which passes through Burton in Kendal, Holme and Milnthorpe en route between Lancaster and Kendal. From Kendal there are services to Windermere and Keswick and to Sedbergh in the Yorkshire Dales. Due to deregulation, services are subject to changes, but Lancashire County Council publishes a range of leaflets describing all the major routes in addition to bus and rail timetables. These may be obtained from;

> Lancashire County Council
> Policy & Public Transport
> Guild House, Cross Street
> Preston PR1 8RD.

An information service on public transport in Lancashire is available on;

> 0870 608 2 608

Operators

> Stagecoach Ribble Information Hotline 01772 886633
> Stagecoach Cumberland timetable enquiries 01946 63222
> Preston Bus Information Centre 01772 821199
> Blackpool Transport 01253 473001

Cycling

For the most part cycling is not allowed on the towpath. However three lengths have been designated as safe for use by bicycles, these being:

> Preston, Ashton Basin,– Br.17 Cottam Hall.
> Millennium Ribble Link (accessible from A583)
> Lancaster, Br. 95 Haverbreaks – Br. 127 Carnforth.
> Carnforth, Canal Basin – Br. 129 Hodgesons.

A permit to cycle the towpath is required, obtainable free by writing to British Waterways, Main Road, Galgate, Lancaster. LA2 0LQ

Visitors fortunate enough to have a cycle with them will find this a useful form of transport for visiting those parts of the county not adequately served by public transport facilities, especially if equipped with the Ordnance Survey maps covering the canal. Unfortunately hiring a cycle is difficult, only the extreme north of the area offering this facility. The northern section of the Lancashire Cycleway provides a loop consisting of 130 miles of way-marked route taking in the Fylde plain, north to Lancaster and the Arnside/Silverdale area before returning south through the Pennines and Forest of Bowland. The route crosses the canal at Bridges 26; 36; 44; 79; 128 and 155. Part of the route between Arnside and Kirkby Lonsdale is

shared with the Cumbria Cycle Way, a circular 259 mile route extending north to Brampton. From Lancaster there are two routes; one to Glasson Dock, the second running eastwards alongside the River Lune as far as Caton Green, both utilising former railways for much of their length. Leaflets describing these routes are obtainable from Tourist Information Centres.

Disabled Access

British Waterways are working towards improving waterways access and have an 'access for all' policy. The improved towpath between Lancaster and Carnforth forms part of this policy. More specific information is available from the Galgate office of British Waterways (Tel: 01524 751888).

TOURIST INFORMATION CENTRES

Kendal	Town Hall, Highgate. Tel: 01539 725758
Lancaster	29 Castle Hill. Tel: 01524 32878
Morecambe	Old Station Buildings, Marine Road Central. Tel: 01524 582808
Preston	The Guild Centre, Lancaster Road. PR1 1HT Tel: 01772 253731
Fleetwood	Freeport Village, FY7 6AE Tel: 01253 777854
Garstang	The Discovery Centre. PR3 1FU Tel: 01995 602125
Blackpool	1 Clifton Street . FY1 1LY Tel: 01253 478222
Lytham St Annes	290 Clifton Drive South. FY8 1LH Tel: 01253 725610

These offices will supply leaflets and up to date opening times for all places of interest mentioned in this guide – plus information on specialist activities. In addition Lancashire County Council operates a number of information centres:

Preston	The Bus Station	Tel: 01772 556618
Fleetwood	15 North Albert Street	Tel: 01253 772704
Lytham	Clifton Square	Tel: 01253 794405

ABOUT THE LANCASTER CANAL TRUST

Formed in 1963, the Lancaster Canal Trust had the prime objective to restore and re-open to navigation, the disused section of the canal from Tewitfield, just north of Carnforth, to Kendal. These plans were thwarted by the Ministry of Transport's proposal to culvert, rather than bridge, the canal in six places, in connection with the northward extension of the M6 motorway. It is fortunate that the canal's engineer, John Rennie, chose a site just south of Kendal at Crooklands as the entry point for the canal's water supply from Killington Reservoir near Sedbergh, otherwise it is unlikely that this length of canal would have survived at all! Despite a six year battle, the Ministry finally won the day for obvious reasons! The commercial traffic on the canal had long since finished and few pleasure craft used the waterway. The farsightedness displayed by the Trust was not shared by the Ministry. Who at that time could have envisaged that by the mid 1970s Britain would witness a second 'canal age', as the intro-duction of fibreglass (G.R.P.) hulled craft at an affordable price for many people, led to thousands of weekend sailors getting afloat on the comparatively safe waters of our canal system.?

Despite these setbacks, the main objective of the Trust is still the restoration of the canal back to Kendal. In recent years the Trust has formed a partnership with the local authorities, British Waterways and other interested groups to form the Northern Reaches Restoration Group. A feasibility study into overcoming the obstacles posed by the motorway has been undertaken and the Group is working towards submitting a bid to the Heritage Lottery Fund to cover a substantial part of the restoration costs. The Trust carries out small scale projects in support of full restoration and operates public trips from Crooklands (Br.166) in a purpose built 28' narrow boat. The Trust has actively supported the work of the Ribble Link Trust in its effort to link the Lancaster Canal to the main cruising network using the River Ribble and the Leeds & Liverpool Canal, thus achieving what John Rennie was not able to do.

Additionally, the Trust supports the development of the canal as a public amenity whilst at the same time seeking to protect the essential character of the canal. The Trust works with the various local authorities and county councils through whose area the canal passes, and with the British Waterways, to extend and improve facilities available to users, whilst at the same time resisting any proposals or developments which would prove injurious to the character and essential environmental features of the canal. Over the years, as a result of the efforts of the Trust, many of the original structures have been protected either as structures of special architectural or scientific interest or by cessfully resisted, notably in Preston, and as a result of the efforts of the Trust many improvements have been made to the towing path and information and interpretive panels have been provided at various sites along the canal. The Trust works in conjunction with various bodies representing the variety of canal users, many of which are affiliated to the Trust. The Trust is affiliated to the Inland Waterways Association and is a registered charity.

We need your help to enable the Trust to achieve its aims and objectives, particularly if we are to be successful in our goal of re-opening the canal to Kendal. All members receive copies of the Trust's magazine, 'Waterwitch', published regularly, which contains information of the work of the Trust and also articles of interest about the canal. Social activities are arranged from time to time and members have the opportunity for practical work through working parties that are arranged in conjunction with British Waterways and crewing the trip boat. Membership details can be found elsewhere in this guide.

The Lancaster Canal Trust would like to thank all the contributors to this Guide and hopes that the value of this publication will be appreciated by all users of the facilities and features of the Canal, both on and off the water.

The Trust gratefully acknowledges a grant towards the cost of this guide by the 'Awards for All' lottery grants programme.

We are particularly appreciative of contributions towards the production costs from our advertisers.

For Information about membership of the Lancaster Canal Trust please contact:
David Slater, 91 Cop Lane, Penwortham, Preston, Lancs PR1 9AH
or visit our web site:
www.hillbeck.f9.co.uk/Lanky/frames.html

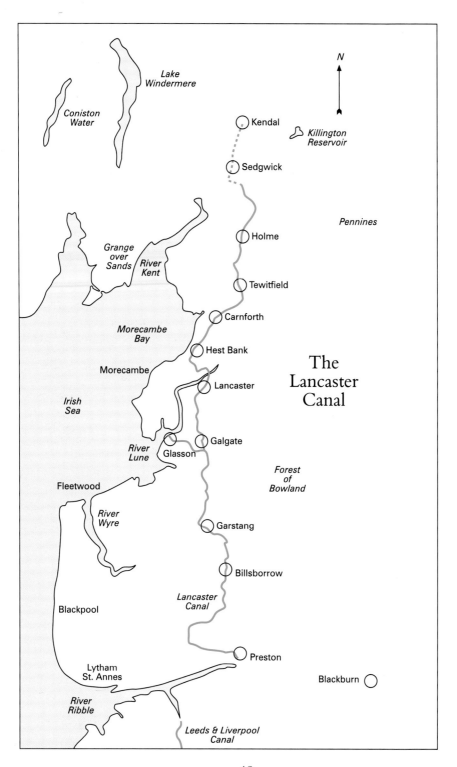

N

Lake
Windermere

Coniston
Water

Kendal

Killington
Reservoir

Sedgwick

Pennines

Holme

Grange
over
Sands

River
Kent

Tewitfield

Carnforth

Morecambe
Bay

Hest Bank

Morecambe

Lancaster

The
Lancaster
Canal

Irish
Sea

Galgate

River
Lune

Glasson

Forest
of
Bowland

Fleetwood

River
Wyre

Garstang

Billsborrow

Blackpool

Lancaster
Canal

Preston

Lytham
St. Annes

Blackburn

River
Ribble

Leeds & Liverpool
Canal

Key

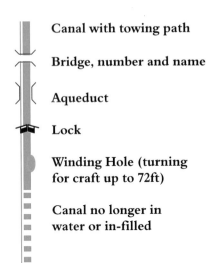

Canal with towing path

Bridge, number and name

Aqueduct

Lock

Winding Hole (turning for craft up to 72ft)

Canal no longer in water or in-filled

Mileage between Kendal *(canal head)* **and Preston** *(original city centre basin)*

B	Boatyard
C	Calor Gas
D	Diesel
G	Garage
I	Information
GS	General Store
M	Visitor Moorings
PH	Public House
Pump	Pump out facilities

PO	Post Office
R	Refuse Disposal
RS	Railway Station
S	BW Sanitary Station
SL	Slipway
T	Telephone
W	Water Point
Sh	Shallow

The maps in this guide follow a route from south to north, starting at the Ribble Link then numbering from Preston (lowest bridge number). When reading the text start at the bottom of each map and work up.

Mileposts can be found at various points along the canal. South of Lancaster they are cast as plates on stone posts and give mileage between Preston and Garstang, and Garstang and Lancaster. North of Lancaster they are engraved stone posts and give mileage between Lancaster and Kendal. Several are missing.

Most bridges on the cruising section are numbered but not named while north of Tewitfield thay are neither numbered or named although we hope this will soon change.

Ordnance Survey coordinates are given for facilities which are not immediately accessible from the canal.

Smart Cards for the BW sanitary stations must be purchased at British Waterways Galgate Office (Tel: 01524 751888)

Cruising Times

Tewitfield										
1.05	Carnforth									
2.00	0.55	Hest Bank								
3.10	2.05	1.10	Lancaster							
4.20	3.15	2.20	1.10	Galgate						
5.10	4.05	3.10	2.00	0.50	Forton					
6.20	5.15	4.20	3.10	2.00	1.10	Garstang				
7.35	6.30	5.35	4.25	3.15	2.25	1.15	Bilsborrow			
8.45	7.40	6.45	5.35	4.25	3.35	2.25	1.10	Catforth		
9.30	8.25	7.30	6.20	5.35	4.20	3.10	1.55	0.45	Salwick	
10.40	9.35	8.40	7.30	6.20	5.30	4.20	3.05	1.55	1.10	Preston

These are minimum times in hours and minutes based on the maximum cruising speed of 4 mph. Actual times will be longer depending on conditions

THE RIBBLE LINK

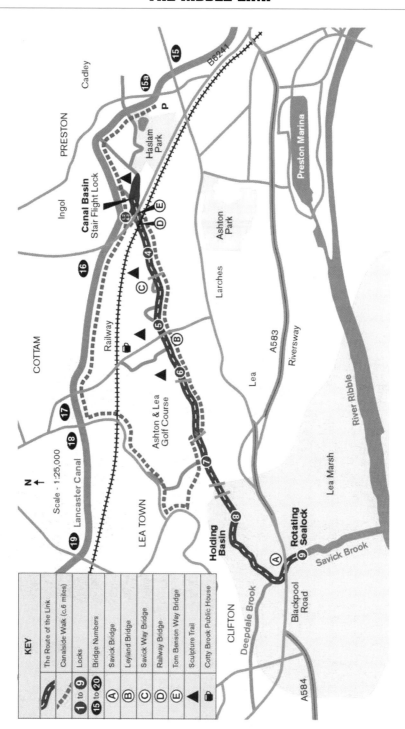

Map courtesy of British Waterways

THE MILLENNIUM RIBBLE LINK

The Millennium Ribble Link is Britain's youngest waterway. The first navigation to be constructed since the Manchester Ship Canal, this new waterway is unique. Built purely for recreation and leisure, the Link was formally opened on 20th September 2002.

The Millennium Ribble Link connects The Lancaster Canal into the Ribble estuary and from there passage is made down the River Douglas to the Rufford Branch of the Leeds and Liverpool Canal. The link consists of nine locks, including a sea lock, known as a 'Rising Sector Gate', which rises to empound the water as the tide goes out. A three-chambered staircase lock flight marks the entrance into the link from the Lancaster canal. Access to the Link is on the towpath side of the Lancaster Canal between bridges 16–16a.

A sculpture trail called 'Gauging the Ripple' has been commissioned along the Link. This four-piece project has attracted a great deal of interest; the four pieces, by sculptor Thompson Dagnall, are named 'Water', 'Earth', 'Fire' and 'Air' and link to the heritage of the waterways.

The Link itself flows along the line of the Savick Brook. This has been canalised, but care has been taken to retain the original bank of the Brook to the north. This has conserved the existing flora and fauna, and the southerly bank is being recolonised quickly. Much of the Link is a wildlife preserve, and BW are looking for funding to manage and develop the remnant wildflower areas. The fish passes which have been constructed are of innovative design, and were developed in partnership with the Environment Agency. The Environment Agency are working with Lancaster Canal staff to produce information boards to be placed on site which explain how fish passes work.

The footpath/nature trail runs from the staircase lock down to lock 8. From this point Blackpool Road can be accessed. Holding basins at both the staircase lock and lock 8 are proving to be an attraction for visitors wanting to see the boats use the Link. Access points for disabled and less mobile people are plentiful, and operational staff can be on hand to provide assistance.

The operation of the Link is the responsibility of the Lancaster Waterway team. With the majority of the feed water coming from the Savick Brook, the Link is liable to rapid changes in water level, so forecasting is an important part of judging whether passage is safe for the boats. Because of weather and tides, the Link will only operate between Easter and October. Passage may occur outside these dates, but it is at the discretion of the Waterway Office. Currently there is no fee for passage but all passages must be pre-booked.

If you wish to navigate the Link contact the Lancaster Waterway office on 01524 751888, or email:
enquiries.LANC@britishwaterways.co.uk or visit the websites:
www.britishwaterways.co.uk or
www.millenniumribblelink.co.uk

It is advisable to contact British Waterways to check on passage availability beforehand as the numbers of craft making the passage at any one time will be strictly controlled. Intending boaters, particularly those coming from the main system to the Lancaster Canal, should be prepared to travel up to Preston dock and await the next available tide if there is is insufficient water in the Savick Brook at the time of arrival. BW staff will direct boats to the dock if this is deemed necessary for safety purposes. A small charge may be made for mooring at Preston Dock.

A towpath has not been provided and therefore mooring will not be allowed other than at times of emergency which will be indicated by red warning signs at the locks. Boaters must moor up at the emergency mooring posts until the situation returns to normal.

The entrance to Savick Brook is on the north bank of the River Ribble, signposts will be provided to aid navigation. Lock 9, which will be operated by BW staff, is the sea passage lock and is unconventional in that it has rotational gates which, when open, lie horizontal in the channel bed when upstream and downstream water levels coincide to allow navigation. When the tide level is at, or below a pre-deter-

22

mined level the gates are in the vertical position to maintain a navigational depth upstream to lock 8.

At certain states of the tide there is insufficient headroom under Savick Bridge which carries the Blackpool Road over the brook. British Waterways will advise on this on arrival at lock 9 and boats will be directed to moor on the floating pontoon upstream of the lock and await further instructions. Boaters travelling downstream from the Lancaster Canal will be advised on passage conditions through Blackpool Road bridge by BW on arrival at lock 8.

Lock 8 is conventional in design and operation but also acts as a sea lock despite being 1½ miles from the River Ribble. The bottom gates are designed to be locked shut to prevent the tide flooding upstream. BW staff will operate this lock.

A footpath and cycleway now runs from the Lancaster Canal as far as lock 8. A pedestrian controlled signalled crossing has been installed to enable walkers to cross Tom Benson Way. The footpath continues via an elevated walkway under the railway line. Care is needed crossing Savick Way and Lea Road. There is no path downstream beyond lock 8 – to reach lock 9 walkers and cyclists will need to

retrace their steps a short distance and take the broad track leading away from the brook and up to Blackpool Road. Although there are footpaths on both sides of Blackpool Road there are no controlled crossing points in the immediate vicinity although negotiations are in hand to allow walkers and cyclists to use the farm access bridge to cross Blackpool Road.

There is no right of way downstream of lock 9. Immediately after Tom Benson Way is a three rise staircase lock. The turn in the lock mouth is very sharp and, to enable craft to enter the bottom lock bow first, a winding hole has been provided to make the turn possible, (see detail map below). Lock 1 opens into a large basin the banks of which have been gently sloped to create a wildlife environment, moorings have been provided on the east side for boats waiting to go down the locks – boats arriving from Savick Brook should continue on to the canal and moor there.

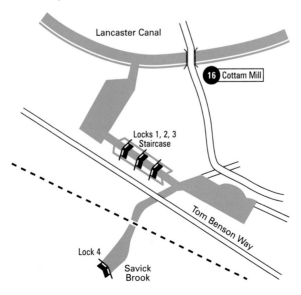

L eaving the Preston City Centre by Fylde Road the Canal commences at Aqueduct Street near its junction with Fylde Road, with pedestrian access to the towpath by one of two footpaths – one from the bottom of Shelley Road and the other from Aqueduct Street itself between the A.T.S. Tyre Specialist and the Ashton Funeral Home. A finger signpost indicates Catforth 7, Garstang 16¼, Tewitfield (cruising terminus) 41¼ and (in the other direction) Preston Town Centre ½ a mile Harris Museum ½ mile. Access to Ashton Basin (approximately 250 metres from the commencement of the canal) is from the mini roundabout 50 metres from the bottom of Tulketh Brow near Wycliffe memorial Church on an unmarked entrance (see details of Ashton basin panel). The entrance also gives access to the canal towpath. The next half mile of canal lies in a cutting surrounded on both sides by housing. Woodplumpton Road crosses the canal at Bridge 12 from where a short walk on the tow path side leads to a shopping centre at Lane Ends – this is also on a bus route. After Bridge 12 Haslam Park opens up on the left whilst on the right are 14 day visitor moorings, refuse disposal facilities and a newly refurbished sanitary station together with picnic and

barbecue area – all on the site of a former coal wharf. Haslam Park offers pleasant walking, municipal bowling greens and tennis courts and a large children's play area.

With the parkland and fields of Haslam Park on the left and houses on the right the canal starts to swing westward, Bridge 13 is the first aqueduct on the canal under which flows Savick Brook. Bridge 14, Hollinghead Fold, is the first of many Rennie 'standard' bridges spanning the canal. Bridge 15, Ingol Ashes, is another but has a pointed parapet rather than a curved one and it is topped with rails. The next bridge, Cottam Mill, is similar but without rails. After Bridge 16 a sign warns of craft entering from the towpath side where the Millennium Ribble Link canal joins the Lancaster Canal and provides access to the Leeds Liverpool Canal and the inland waterway network. (see previous page).

Just after Bridge 16a the new Preston Sports Arena (Tel: 01772 761000) is situated which provides pitches and courts for most sports, together with changing facilities, etc. The Arena extends almost to Bridge 18. The main entrance to the Arena for boaters is at Bridge 17 where mooring is provided. Bridge 17,

PRESTON

Preston is the country's newest city, being granted such status in 2002. It was the coming of the canal, quickly followed by the railway, which transformed Preston from a market into an industrial town and port, particularly important during the boom years of the Lancashire cotton industry. This resulted in town being completely remodelled and none of the buildings are more than 200 years old. Preston's growth was such that it eclipsed Lancaster, the old county town and it is now the administrative centre for Lancashire. The cotton magnates bequeathed many fine buildings, notably the Town Hall and the Harris Library & Museum, located on the flag market. Also of note is the Guildhall, a modern building, also containing the Charter Theatre.

The shopping area contains all the usual high street names plus a wide variety of eating and drinking establishments catering for all tastes. while the town still retains its past in the open and covered markets. The majority of shops are located along Fishergate and in the Fishergate and St George's Centres. Just off Fishergate can be found Winckley Square a fine collection of

Georgian and Edwardian property. Now mostly used commercially, this was the place to live for Preston's gentry, and it is not difficult to imagine how life must have been in Victorian times. Just beyond, to the south, lie the the two gems of Preston's many parks. Avenham and Miller Parks with wide open expanses sweeping down to the Ribble. The parks are well worth a visit if only to trace the route of the tramroad and to view the replica bridge that carried it across the Ribble.

The town planners in Preston must wish they had the benefit of hindsight and that they had retained the canal in the town centre. The canal now starts about a mile and half to the north, at Ashton Basin from where buses run frequently into the city. All services from this area start and terminate at the bus station and are operated mainly by Preston Bus – have plenty of small change available as change is not given on these buses. The bus station is a short walk from Lancaster Road and the Harris Museum, through St John's shopping centre. The tourist information centre is located on Lancaster Road at the entrance to the Guildhall complex.

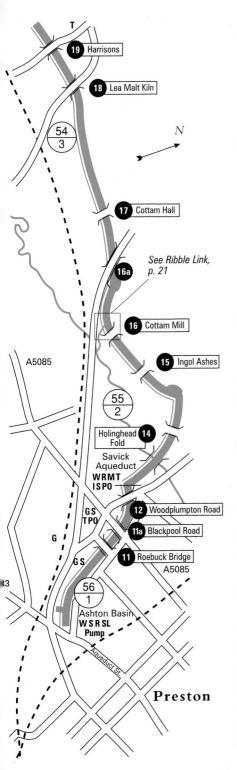

Cottam Hall, is a skew Rennie standard – not a common type on the Lancaster Canal as most are at 90 degrees to the water channel. Between Bridges 16a and 18 on the right of the canal at Cottam new housing has been built with a pub and school and extensively landscaped areas which include a canalside walk, small children's play area and a pier with a signpost stating Lancaster Canal: Preston 2½ miles, Tewitfield 40 miles. Lea Road crosses the canal at Bridge 18 – Lea Malt Kiln Bridge. The houses finally peter out and beyond lies open countryside with the only the railway line intruding.

Cyclists may join the official cycle way at Ashton Basin (off Tulketh Brow) or the access ramp in Haslam Park and exit at Cottam Hall Bridge (No. 17).

PUBS

There are numerous pubs in Preston.
The following can be found close to the canal.

The Lime Kiln, at the commencement of the canal. Down-to-earth, one-room pub serving traditional beers and bar lunches, 12 noon to 2.00 pm.

The Ancient Oak, Merrytrees Lane, Cottam, approx 1.6 km from Bridge 17 offside. Children's play area. Food 12 noon to 10.00 pm.

Saddle Inn, Bartle. Bridge 19 offside 1 km. Bear left at first junction. SD 487 327. Bar meals lunch & evening. Last food orders 9.00 pm (8.00 pm on Sunday). Children welcome, play area. Traditional Thwaites best mild & bitter.

Sitting Goose, Bartle. 400 m past Saddle Inn. SD 486 330. Bar meals lunch & evening, Children welcome until 8.45 pm. Traditional Thwaites best mild & bitter.

The City of Preston is home to a number of museums with exhibitions and activities for the whole family. There is a good selection of shopping centres and a choice of multiplex cinemas.

Harris Museum & Art Gallery, Tel: 01772 258248. Free, city centre, closed Sunday & Bank Holidays.

Museum of Lancashire, Tel: 01772 264075. Admission Charge, city centre, closed Sunday, Thursday & Bank Holidays.

National Football Museum, Tel: 01772 908442. Admission charge, Deepdale Stadium, closed Sunday & Monday (except BH).

Queens Lancashire Regiment Museum, Tel: 01772 260362. Free, Fulwood Barracks, open Tuesday, Wednesday, Thursday.

The canal continues westwards through open country, with the railway in close proximity. The only intrusion on an otherwise rural landscape is the Springfields plant of BNFL, which manufactures fuel rods for our nuclear power stations. The small cluster of buildings on the left is Lea Town which has a pub, and can be reached from bridge 22. As you approach bridge 24, the canal starts to swing north, passing Salwick Hall (not open to the public) on the right, from bridge 25 it is a short walk to Salwick Station. Just beyond bridge 25 lies Salwick Wharf which once served the market town of Kirkham and is now a popular mooring spot, The great loop that the canal traverses was made to accommodate a projected canal to Fleetwood and the coast, which never reached fruition. Past Salwick Wharf, the canal enters a deep cutting for the next half mile and is best seen in Autumn. Bridge 27 is known as Six Mile Bridge and a

nearby milestone indicates that on original mileage, you are now six miles from Preston.

Salwick Moss Bridge (no. 28) used to be nick-named New Bridge, because it replaced a former lift bridge. The canal heads due north, passing under the M55 motorway. From bridge 29, a fine view west across the rural Fylde plain can be seen, the most striking feature being the many radio masts of RNWS Inskip, a communications centre for the Ministry of Defence. From bridge 30, a short walk to Catforth Gardens and Nursery, open April – September.

At bridge 32 there is a busy and attractive family boatyard housed in the old canal cottages and stables. From bridge 28 – 32 boaters may find overnight noise from the M55 intrusive.

The village of **Catforth**, where petrol may be obtained, lies one mile north of bridge 31.

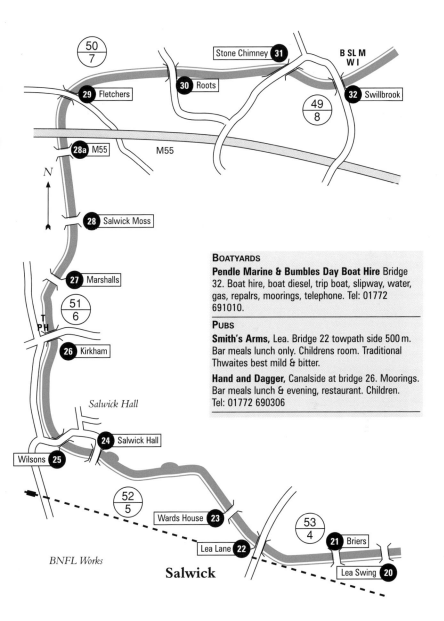

BOATYARDS

Pendle Marine & Bumbles Day Boat Hire Bridge 32. Boat hire, boat diesel, trip boat, slipway, water, gas, repairs, moorings, telephone. Tel: 01772 691010.

PUBS

Smith's Arms, Lea. Bridge 22 towpath side 500 m. Bar meals lunch only. Childrens room. Traditional Thwaites best mild & bitter.

Hand and Dagger, Canalside at bridge 26. Moorings. Bar meals lunch & evening, restaurant. Children. Tel: 01772 690306

Bridge 33 is in fact an aqueduct carrying the canal over Woodplumpton Brook and is worth a closer look. There were originally 22 aqueducts on the canal, all designed by John Rennie. One has since been destroyed and another replaced. No two are alike and the traveller should stop and examine the larger ones as they represent fine examples of canal building. Woodplumpton village itself is best reached from bridge 35 or 36 The churchyard is reputed to contain the body of a witch. This can be identified by the large boulder covering the grave so, as legend has it, to prevent the witch from digging her way out.

Bridge 37 is a swing bridge, one of only three built on this canal, and must be normally left in the open position. One bridge has disappeared, the other remaining being Hatlex Swing Bridge, at Hest Bank, which is normally shut against the canal. Just beyond lies Hollowforth Mill, now a private residence, but once a water mill. Hollowforth Aqueduct (bridge 38) is an interesting three arch structure and one may walk through the northernmost arch. From bridge 39 it is just

over a mile to the village of Barton where there are restaurantsand a hotel and garden centre, about one mile east of the bridge. There are bus services back to Preston or north to Garstang and Lancaster. The canal now enters an entirely rural landscape, remote from major roads. From bridge 42 it is a short walk to White Horse on the A6 where there is a pub, garage, post office and telephone. The village of Bilsborrow is marked on some maps as Duncombe. A mile west of bridge 44 lies the campus of the Lancashire College of Agriculture and Horticulture which is open to the public on certain days. Just before bridge 45, the canal widens into a basin. Petrol may be obtained from a garage on the A6, a short distance away. 14 day Visitor Moorings Br. 44 – 45.

Woodplumpton: *PO; Tel; Stores.* A half mile south of bridge 35.

Bilsborrow: *PO; Tel; Stores; Garage.* A village built along the A6 which is much quieter than before the M6 arrived. There are three pubs here.

Boatyards

Moons Bridge Marina, Bridge 36. Boat Hire, water, gas, diesel, shop, chandlery, moorings. Tel: 01772 690627.

Pubs

Plough at Eaves, Woodplumpton. Bridge 35 offside 1km. SD 501 345. Bar meals lunch & Wed to Sat evenings. Buffet Sun. Children's play area. Traditional Theakstons mild & bitter.

Boar's Head, Barton. Bridge 39 offside 1km. SD 517 362. Restaurant all day. Children until 9pm. Traditional Whitbread Castle Eden Ale.

White Horse, Barton. Bridge 42 offside 600 m. Bar meals lunch & evening. Children lunch only. Traditlonal Theakstons mild & bitter.

Owd Nell's Restaurant & Guy's Eating Establishment, Canalside bridge 44, housed together in a thatched building. **Owd Nell's** has Bar meals lunch & evening. Children. Traditional Whitbread Castle Eden Ale, Chester's mild & bitter, Boddington's bitter plus guest beers. Hotel, tearooms and retail outlet. Tel 01995 640010/640020

White Bull, Canalside between bridges 44 & 45. Bar meals. Traditional Theakstons mild & bitter.

Roebuck, Opposite the White Bull across the A6. Bar meals lunch & evening. Children. Traditional Theakstons mild & bitter.

Olde Duncombe Guest House, Canalside at bridge 44. B&B accomodation. Tel 01995 40336.

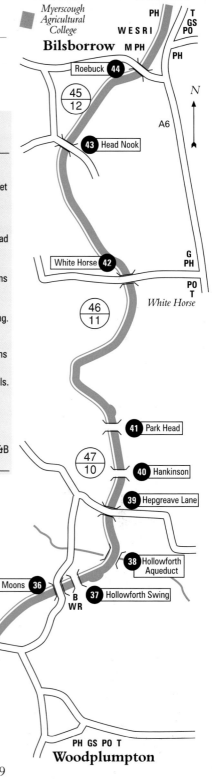

The Brock Aqueduct is the first major river crossing since leaving Preston and is worth closer examination. Due to the nature of the topography, the canal builders were forced to lower the level of the river in order to build the aqueduct of sufficient strength, and to construct a weir on the upstream side. At this point, there is an uninterupted view of the Bowland Fells, Parlick and Fairsnape, whilst a little further south lies the lower tree-clad summit of Beacon Fell, now a country park. From Beacon Fell on a clear day one can view the whole of the Fylde plain and the coast. From Brock Aqueduct, the canal turns east for a short distance and then runs close to the M6 and the railway. The strange Dalek-like structure on the towpath side, just north of Bridge 48, is a borehole wellhead, many of which can be seen in the area. There is a garage and small shop on the A6 by bridge 49. Claughton Park is the estate of the Brockholes family whose residence Claughton Hall lies a mile to the east. When the railway was being built, the then encumbent of the Hall insisted the railway company built a decorative bridge. Though much altered as a result of electrification, the badger emblem of the family may still be seen. On the approach to Catterall, the canal passes through a pleasant wooded stretch. The house on the left just before bridge 51 has been converted from a former stable for the horses and attendants for the passenger boat service, horses being changed every four miles. Bridge 52 is the Calder Aqueduct, another example of a river having been lowered to accommodate the canal and north of bridge 53 one may discern the feeder entering the canal from the River Calder at the basin. It is difficult to imagine that this was an important little industrial area but nothing remains to testify to it's past. The remains of Garstang and Catterall station on

the main line, once the junction of the branch line through Garstang to Pilling and Knott End on the coast, is passed by bridge 54. Unfortunately both branch line and station closed many years ago and there is very little left to see. About 2 miles along the lane east at bridge 54 lies the sleepy village of Caldervale, nestling in the valley of the River Calder. The western flank of the Pennines is now visible to the east. Bridge 57 is the place from which to inspect the remains of Greenhalgh Castle, built by the Earl of Derby in 1490. During The Civil War, the castle was held for the King and was almost the last place to hold out against the Parliamentary forces.

Catterall: *PO; Tel; Stores.* Half mile west of bridge 51. A small village spread out along the old A6 turnpike.

Claughton Hall: One mile east of bridge 51. An Elizabethan Mansion originally built beside Claughton Parish Church, a quarter of a mile to the east. It was moved lock, stock and barrel to its present site in the 1930s. SD 523 425. It is now the residence of the Brockholes family.

PUBS

Brock Tavern, *Brock.* Bridge 47 300 m south on A6. Keg beers and restaurant.

Brockholes Arms, *Catterall.* Bridge 51 towpath side 1km. SD 502 425. Bar meals lunch. Children lunch only.

Kenlis Arms, *Catterall.* Bridge 54 offside 200 m. Lunchtime & Evening meals. Tel: 01995 603307.

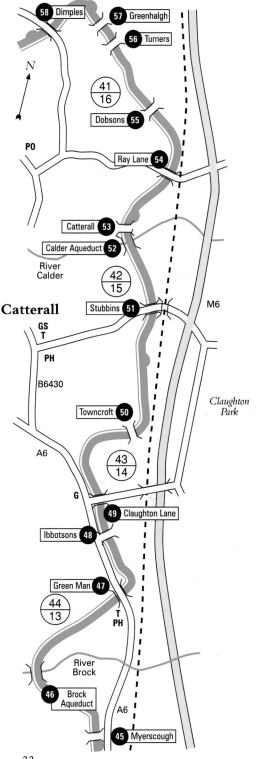

You are now on the outskirts of Garstang but as the canal skirts round the south-west side of this small town, urbanisation does not intrude. The River Wyre is crossed on a majestic single arch aqueduct with the river thirty feet below. The aqueduct is best viewed from the footpath running along the river bank which can be accessed from the towing path. Just beyond lies Garstang basin. The building on the north side is a Tithe Barn, predating the canal by over a hundred years and built of brick, a rarely used material at that time. The building is now used as a restaurant. Many old industrial and agricultural artefacts hang from the roof and walls of the barn. Mooring is available opposite the basin on the towpath side. From here it is a couple of minutes walk to the town centre. Visitor Moorings, bridge 61 – 62. The pipe bridge to the north of Garstang carries water from Barnacre Reservoir to Blackpool and the Fylde. 300m south of Bridge 63b there is a farm store. At bridge 64 there is a handy shop selling homemade pies, pastries and sandwiches, 8.00 am – 3.00 pm Mon – Sat. The canal passes quickly back into rural Lancashire. On the offside is Bridge House Marina with all facilities for boaters. A little further north is the dismantled 'Pilling Pig' railway line which was a railway running from Garstang to Knott End at the mouth of the River Wyre. One mile west of bridge 68 is Winmarleigh Hall, a stately mansion surrounded by trees and a former home of Lord Winmarleigh. It is now owned by Lancashire County Council and is used as an institute of agriculture. Petrol may be obtained from the garage at bridge 71. The canal continues to wind through the countryside, hugging the 70 foot contour. The canalsides are rich with yellow flag, yellow water lily and watermint. A few miles to the offside are the windswept fells of the Forest of Bowland, which rise to 561 metres at Ward's Stone.

Garstang *PO; Tel; Shops; Banks; Tourist Information and Heritage Centre Tel. 01995 602125.* A charming market town, one of the most important in Lancashire and mentioned in the Domesday Book. The 18th century Church of St. Thomas is near bridge 62. The interesting little Town Hall was rebuilt in 1939 to replace the original 1680 building which was constructed when King Charles II conferred Borough status on the town. There is a good selection of shops, including supermarkets, hardware stores and a garden centre. There is a market on Thursday on the cobbled market place and up the High Street. Buses run from here to Preston, Blackpool and Lancaster. Trip Boat 'Ashanti Gold'; tel: 01772 633362.

St. Helens Church 2 miles south of Garstang. Anyone interested in churches should visit this ancient parish church, known as The Cathedral of the Fylde, and situated in an attractive setting near the River Wyre at Churchtown, a short bus ride from Garstang. Most of the structure is 15th century but parts are Norman in origin. The roof beams are made from 4 oaks that Henry IV gave to Churchtown when forests were still the property of the crown.

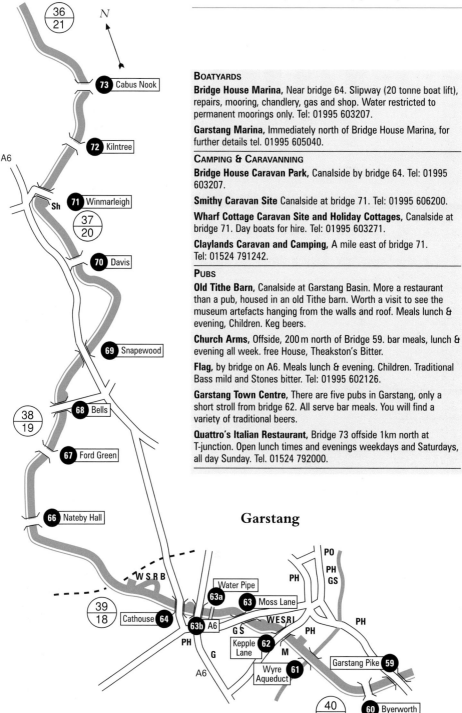

BOATYARDS

Bridge House Marina, Near bridge 64. Slipway (20 tonne boat lift), repairs, mooring, chandlery, gas and shop. Water restricted to permanent moorings only. Tel: 01995 603207.

Garstang Marina, Immediately north of Bridge House Marina, for further details tel. 01995 605040.

CAMPING & CARAVANNING

Bridge House Caravan Park, Canalside by bridge 64. Tel: 01995 603207.

Smithy Caravan Site Canalside at bridge 71. Tel: 01995 606200.

Wharf Cottage Caravan Site and Holiday Cottages, Canalside at bridge 71. Day boats for hire. Tel: 01995 603271.

Claylands Caravan and Camping, A mile east of bridge 71. Tel: 01524 791242.

PUBS

Old Tithe Barn, Canalside at Garstang Basin. More a restaurant than a pub, housed in an old Tithe barn. Worth a visit to see the museum artefacts hanging from the walls and roof. Meals lunch & evening, Children. Keg beers.

Church Arms, Offside, 200 m north of Bridge 59. bar meals, lunch & evening all week. free House, Theakston's Bitter.

Flag, by bridge on A6. Meals lunch & evening. Children. Traditional Bass mild and Stones bitter. Tel: 01995 602126.

Garstang Town Centre, There are five pubs in Garstang, only a short stroll from bridge 62. All serve bar meals. You will find a variety of traditional beers.

Quattro's Italian Restaurant, Bridge 73 offside 1km north at T-junction. Open lunch times and evenings weekdays and Saturdays, all day Sunday. Tel. 01524 792000.

Garstang

The Annual Lancaster Easter

MARITIME FESTIVAL

(Good Friday – Easter Monday)

Featuring the World's biggest gathering of Sea Song and Shanty performers

Supported by a wide array of Maritime themed entertainments

Lancaster City Council
Arts & Events Service
Old Station Buildings,
Morecambe, LA4 4DB
tel: **01524 586822**

And Remember! Beware the Press Gang

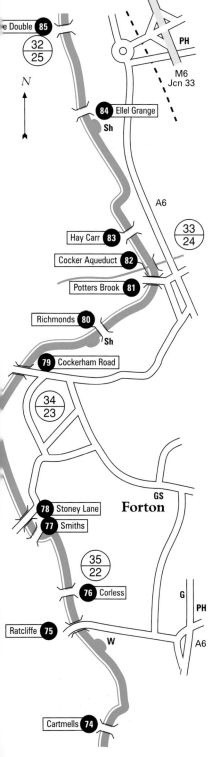

Just prior to Ratcliffe Bridge (No. 75) on the off-side is Ratcliffe Wharf. This was once busy with canal barges and is now a mooring. The mounds behind the mooring are old lime kilns, which were common along the length of the canal. Barges would bring in limestone and coal, and the lime was burnt. The burnt 'Quicklime' was used to improve farmland and to make mortar. North of bridge 75 is perhaps the most beautiful stretch of the canal. Notice the number of small canalside woodlands. Most were originally planted with larch to provide timber for canal related works. Some larch remain, characterised by their swooping branches and curved needles. Forton lies a mile south-east of bridge 79. It became the richest village in England due to the payments received when the M6 motorway was built. The small basin at Richmond Bridge was constructed for transhipment of stone from the nearby quarry which is now disused. At bridge 84 is Ellel Grange, built between 1857 and 1859. The bridge is more ornate in style, in keeping with that of the secluded mansion. The next bridge along (No. 85) is Double Bridge. The bridge was to lie at the boundary between two farms, so the Canal Company had to build a 'double' bridge with accesses divided by a wall.

CAMPING AND CARAVANING
Six Arches Caravan Park, A mile east of bridge 74. SD 496 494. Tel: 01524 791683.

PUBS
New Holly Forton, Bridge 75 offside 1km east on A6 (bear left at T-junction). Bar meals lunch & evening. Children's room. Accommodation. Traditional Thwaites best mild & bitter.

Bay Horse, Bridge 81 offside 500 m. First left, across cross-roads. Bar meals lunch (not Mon) & evenings (Sat & Sun). Children. Traditional mild & bitter.

Hampson House, Bridge 84 offside 1km. Turn north up A6 then East before M6 Jn. Hotel. Restaurant. Bar meals. Free House.

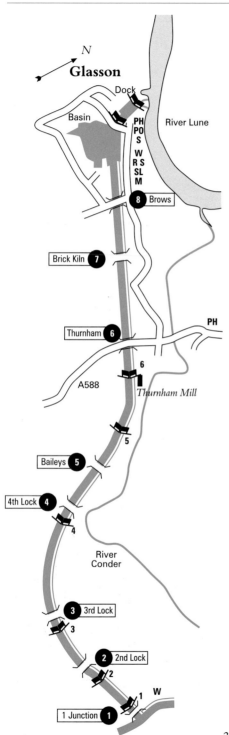

The junction with the Glasson Branch is marked by the lock keeper's cottage and a turnover bridge. The branch was not opened until 1826 although it provided a vital link to the sea, There are six locks to Glasson Basin, with another down to Glasson Dock. To use the lock between the Basin and the Dock you should contact British Waterways Galgate Office, tel 01524 751888, at least 24hrs beforehand. The top gates of the locks are padlocked for security reasons. The lock gates should be shut after use and the lock should be left empty, even when ascending. The flight gently descends to the sea, following the line of the River Conder which runs into the River Lune at Glasson. There are good views around, especially to the slopes of Clougha Pike. Close to Bridge 4 is Thurnham Hall, which is now a timeshare complex, with its chapel and woodlands. Close to Lock 6 is Thurham Mill. This was at one time fed by canal water – the old mill can be seen next to the towing path. The canal company purchased the mill in 1824 for £1,100 in order to obtain its right to take water from the River Conder and divert it into the canal and thence to the mill wheel, the tail race returning the water to the canal below the lock. The old mill has been restored and is now a hotel and restaurant. The canal ends at the basin which served as a reservoir for the outer dock at low tides. It is now full of sea-going yachts. There is a large boatyard and British Waterways Visitor Moorings. At one time, small sea-going vessels sailed up the canal to Kendal and Preston. Sea-going craft can go through the dock and sea lock out onto the Lune Estuary, and thence to the Irish Sea. It is also possible to travel up the River Lune to Lancaster if the tide conditions are right, although this is not recommended for canal craft. The sea lock can be used 1 hour before high water. 24 hours notice should be given to British Waterways Galgate Office, tel 01524 751888.

Glasson: The canal, which was completed in 1826, leads into Glasson Basin. This covers twelve acres and could accomodate 200 ton sea-going vessels. The basin now shelters ocean-going yachts and is used for wind surfing. Glasson Dock, as part of the Port of Lancaster, was opened in 1787. Grain and timber were the main imports and coal to Ireland was the main export. The opening of Preston Dock in 1892 brought Glasson's period of greatness to an end and it has settled down to the quiet place it is today, although it still serves coasters from Britain and abroad. There are many delightful walks near the Lune Estuary and those to nearby Cockersand Abbey to the south, and the 4 mile footpath walk along the Lune Estuary to Lancaster should not be missed. Glasson Village includes pubs and shops and is built round the dock.

Thurnham Hall, A half mile south of bridge 6. A battlemented 16th century Mansion, once the family home of the Daltons.

CAMPING AND CARAVANING

Marina Camping and Caravan Park, Canalside at bridge 7. Tel: 01524 751787.

BOATYARDS

Glasson Basin Yacht Co., Slipway, dry dock, repairs, moorings, crane, chandlery, water and sanitary station. Tel: 01524 751491.

PUBS

Stork, Conder Green. Bridge 6 towpath side 500 m north. Bar meals lunch & evening. Children. Accommodation. Traditional Thwaites mild & bitter. Tel: 01524 751234

Victoria, North corner of basin. Bar meals lunch & evening. Children. Guest ales.

Thurnham Mill by lock 6, hotel and restaurant. tel. 01524 752852

Dalton Arms, by the dock, 200 m from basin. Bar meals lunch & evening. Children. Traditional Thwaites bitter.

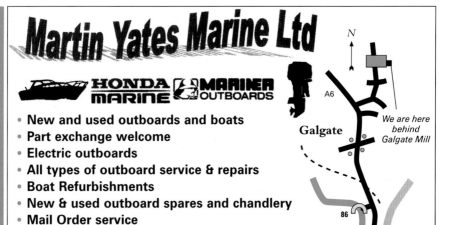

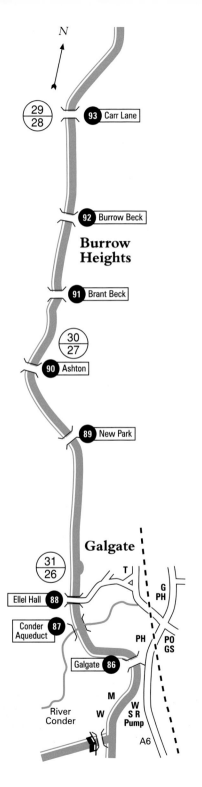

Half a mile north of Glasson Junction is the small village of Galgate. The canal skirts around Galgate and after passing over the River Conder Aqueduct, enters rather flat country until it reaches Brant Beck Bridge (No. 91) where it enters Burrow Heights Cutting, more familiarly known as Deep Cutting. This was built through glacial deposits in order to avoid a long detour. The cutting is up to 10 metres deep and over 2 km long. The gateway to the southern end of the cutting is majestic. Beyond Brantbeck Bridge the canal quietly winds through woodland, the best area on the canal to see kingfishers. The northern end of Deep Cutting is marked by a view to Lancaster Castle. Bargees know this as 'Hangman's Corner' – apparently condemned prisoners being exercised here gave it that name.

Galgate: *PO; Tel; Stores; Garage.* A town dominated by the railway which passes through on a tall viaduct. A useful place to stop for provisions or refreshment. It also has a handy Fish and Chip shop. The Mill on the east of the town was the oldest silk mill in England and has now been converted to industrial units. From Galgate there is a good footpath, partly along the canal, to Glasson Dock 2 miles to the west. Visitor Moorings Br 85 – 86.

BOATYARDS

Marina Park Services, Bridge 86. Boat sales. Tel: 01524 751368. Now also houses B.W. Lancaster Waterway Office tel. 01524 751888 and card operated sanitary station. *Note: Smart cards for this sanitary station and the one at Aldcliffe Wharf, Lancaster, can only be purchased here.*

PUBS

Plough Inn, Galgate. Bridge 86 offside 50 m. Meals all day, beer garden, guest beers.

Green Dragon, Galgate. Bridge 86 offside 200 m. Bar meals lunch & evening. B&B. Children. Traditional Thwaite's best mild & bitter.

New Inn, Galgate. Bridge offside 250 m. Bar meals lunch & evening. Children. Boddingtons bitter.

Passing under the main line railway, bridge 97, one soon arrives at the old packet-boat house and adjoining wharf. This was used for repairing packet or passenger boats between 1833 and 1843. The building held two boats with workshops above. It contained a hoist by which boats could be lifted to the upper floors. Note that the front is skewed – this allowed the launching of these long thin boats. Just north of the former BW yard with its facilities is one of the few turnover bridges on the canal (No. 98). These allowed the horse towing the barge to change sides of the canal, without unhitching. Years of wear by the tow ropes has resulted in an iron bridge plate on the towing path side being badly worn. Beyond Bridge 98 are two large canal basins and the Waterwitch public house, which used to be canal stables. The basins were originally covered and were used for the loading/unloading of barges. This is the best place to moor and discover the city of Lancaster. Visitor Moorings The canal passes canalside mills, many of which have been put to new use, as offices and housing. Between Bridges 102 and 103 are excellent views over the city and to the castle and priory on the hill. The canal winds north from Lancaster then suddenly turns left across Bulk Aqueduct over the main road to the M6. Rennie's original narrow stone structure was replaced in 1961 to allow road widening. The canal continues along a huge embankment to the Lune Aqueduct.

THE LUNE AQUEDUCT

"To public Prosperity – Old needs are served; Far distant sites combined; Rivers by art to bring new wealth are joined."

Lune Aqueduct The aqueduct was formally opened on 22nd November 1797. It took five years to build and cost £48,000. It stands on wooden piles, driven twenty feet into the river bed and is 5l feet (15.5m) above the river and 664 feet(202m) long. Designed by Rennie and built from local stone, it is considered to be one of the most beautiful aqueducts in the country and is a listed building. It is certainly the finest piece of engineering on the Lancaster Canal.

Lancaster This historic city and port still retains much of its character. It was originally the site of a Roman fortress and a crossing of the River Lune but it was only created a city by King George VI on 14th May 1937. Lancaster was the home of the House of Lancaster and John O'Gaunt's statue dominates the City from over the castle gateway. A shoe, reputedly from his horse, can be seen cast into one of the paving stones in Market Street. Bonnie Prince Charlie made his headquarters in the town during the Jacobite Rebellion. Lancaster was once a thriving port and the old canal quays are now providing sites for new student accommodation for Lancaster University.

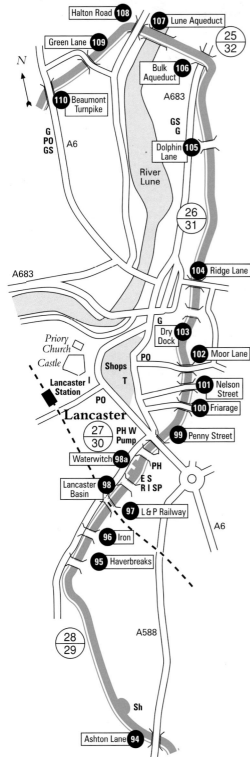

Cyclists may now join the official cycleway at Beaumont bridge (No. 110) and exit at Haverbreaks bridge (No. 95). Mooring rings available and canalside seats between bridges 100 and 101. Public seats and dog loos available between Bridges 101 and 102.

River Lune Millennium Park

Rennie's impressive aqueduct not only crosses the Lune but also the newly created River Lune Millennium Park. A footpath/cycleway has been created from a disused railway line running inland on the southern bank of the river from St George's Quay as far as just east of Caton at Bull Beck. Access is via a flight of steps off the towpath just south of the aqueduct. The riverside is the best place to gauge the magnitude of the structure. Passing under the aqueduct the remnants of industry that developed with the coming of the railway are evident but this ends as you pass beneath the impressive single arched span of the motorway bridge. A little further and the remains of station are reached connected to the village on the opposite bank of the river by a cast iron bridge. After Halton the valley narrows into a deep wooded gorge the river running deep past the remains of former mills on the opposite bank. Had Brindley's original survey for the canal been followed it would have crossed the river at this point. The Crook O'Lune must be one of the most delightful spots in Lancashire if not England. Turner certainly thought so since he painted the scene from the viewpoint at Gray's Seat reached by a short detour. The river makes a horseshoe loop at this point the path crossing the river twice within a few hundred yards. The area has been designated a country park; car parking toilets and information panels are provided for the visitor. The walker may choose to return to the canal by following a series of footpaths on the north bank of the river, although this route involves some road walking. *Continued on next page*

43

The Millennium Park features public works of art and interpretive panels along its length. A descriptive leaflet is available from the Lancaster Tourist Information Centre. There is a website: www.lancaster.gov.uk/millennium. Those whose legs give up will be pleased to know that buses run through Caton into Lancaster, passing beneath the canal at Bulk Aqueduct (Br. 106).

Lancaster Castle An impressive fortress, built mainly in the 13th and 14th centuries, set on the heights overlooking the city. It has a Norman Keep and a beacon tower known as John of Gaunt's seat. A drawing of the John O'Gaunt gateway was used by the original Lancaster Canal Company for it's seal. The Shire Hall has an extensive collection of heraldic shields. This is now the county court and a prison. The famous Pendle witches were tried here. It is open daily from Good Friday to the end of September, except when the courts are in session. **Priory Church,** Castle Hill. Built between 1380 and 1430. Open daily. **Penny's Hospital Almshouses** built in 1720. **Judges Lodgings** houses the Museum of Childhood, built in 1675. Open from Easter to October. **Cottage Museum** 15, Castle Hill built 1739. Go back in time to see how life was in 1825. Open summer afternoons. **Maritime Museum** St. George's Quay. Open daily. Includes canal history and a full-size replica of the packet boat 'Waterwitch'. **Williamson Park** An attractive Park containing an ornamental lake, Palm House, the Butterfly House with its fascinating collection of tropical butterflies, and the **Ashton Memorial**, an amazing Edwardian Folly. **Lancaster Museum** Market Street. Prehistoric, Roman and Mediaeval exhibits. **Theatre and Cinema The Dukes**, Moor Lane, provides live theatre and also film shows. Lancaster Footlights also provide regular performances at the **Grand Theatre**, St. Leonardgate. There is also a twin cinema in King Street.

Morecambe and Heysham, a short train or bus ride from Lancaster. Morecambe is a scaled down version of Blackpool but is set in the attractive surrounds of Morecambe Bay.

Heysham Village This has a quaint main street and is famous for its Nettle Beer. The port of Heysham runs a passenger ferry service to the Isle of Man and Ireland.

PUBS

Waterwitch, Bridge 98a canalside. Bar meals lunch & evening. Children. Traditional Thwaite's mild & bitter, McEwan's 70/-, Bass, Stone's bitter, Tetley's mild & bitter.

Farmer's Arms, Bridge 99 offside 50m. Bar meals lunch & evening. Children. Accommodation. Thwaites best mild & bitter.

Revolution, Bridge 99 offside 50 m. Bar meals until 8pm. Children lunch only.

White Cross, Canalside between bridges 99 & 100. Bar meals & restaurant lunch & evening. Traditional Bass draught & mild, Stone's bitter.

Slyne Lodge, Bridge 118 offside 1km. Across crossroads, left at T-junction. SD 477 651. Bar meals and restaurant lunch & evening. Children. Accommodation. Traditional Hartley's bitter Theakston's bitter, Tetley's bitter.

There are also numerous pubs in the centre of Lancaster, which is best reached from bridge 99. There is also a selection of restaurants and the usual fast food establishments.

Filling Station, shops, PO, launderette, fish & chips, bus connections adjacent bridge 110.

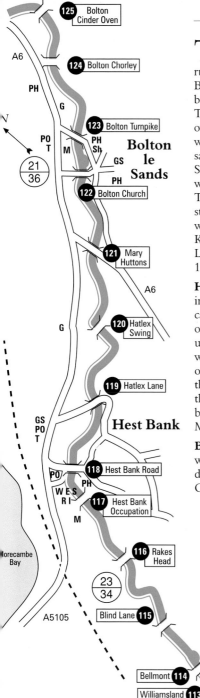

The canal runs northwards into pleasant countryside with views across to Morecambe Bay. At Hest Bank, the canal runs very near to Morecambe Bay. Before the Glasson Branch was built in 1826, goods were trans shipped here between sailing boats in Morecambe Bay and canal barges, The Hest Bank Hotel lay on the coaching route to Grange-over-Sands on the opposite side of the bay. A light in the window facing the canal would guide coachmen across the sands. After Hest Bank, the canal passes through Bolton-le-Sands, a pleasant village close to the sea. The Packet Boat Inn was one of the stopping points for passenger 'packet' boats. There would have been a landing stage on the offside and steps up to the inn. From 1833, a special swift packet service was run, completing the round trip between Preston and Kendal in a day. The service was withdrawn in 1846 when the Lancaster and Carlisle Railway was opened. Adjacent to Br. 115 is the site of a ruined packet boat stables.

Hest Bank: *PO; Tel; Stores.* Once busy with canal boats and inland vessels, this is now a suburb of Lancaster and More-cambe. It is the nearest the canal comes to the sea, which is only a few hundred yards away at high water. The sands are uncovered at low water and in summer there are guided walks across them to Kents Bank, six miles on the other side of the Bay. Details of guided walks available at the café on the foreshore. On no account should visitors venture across the sands without a guide.There are opportunities here for birdwatching (refer to RSPB tel. 01524 701601). Visitor Moorings, Br. 116–117.

Bolton-le-Sands: *PO; Tel; Stores.* An attractive village which takes pride in its canal, with many gardens landscaped down to the water. Visitor Moorings, Packet Bridge Fish & Chips adjacent Bridge 123.

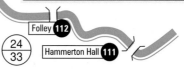

CAMPING AND CARAVANING
Sandside Camping & Caravan Site, a half mile north-west of bridge 122. SD 475 685. Tel: 01524 822311.
Detron Gate Caravan Site, Tel 01524 732842.

PUBS
Hest Bank Hotel, Canalside bridge 118. Bar meals, lunchtimes & evening. Children. Traditional Boddington's.
Blue Anchor, Main St, Bolton-le-Sands. Bridge 122 offside 100m. Bar meals. Children. Traditional beers.
Packet Boat Hotel, Main St, Bolton- le-Sands. Bridge 123 offside 50m. Meals, lunch & evening. Children. Thwaites. Tel: 01524 822289.
Royal Hotel, Bolton-le-Sands. Br. 124 towpathside, 100m left on A6. Bar meals, lunch. Children. Traditional beers.

45

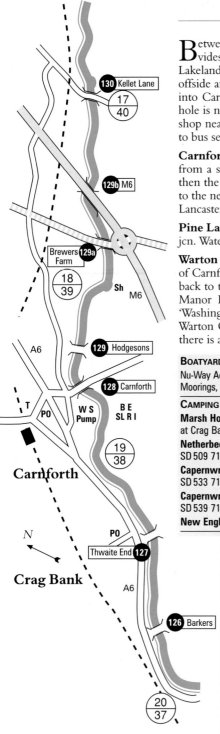

Between Bolton-le-Sands and Tewitfield the canal provides excellent views across Morecambe Bay to the Lakeland mountains. Close to Thwaite End Bridge on the offside are the remains of lime kilns (private). Passing north into Carnforth there is a large winding hole. The winding hole is now the site of Nu-Way Acorn. There is a BP garage shop nearby on the A6 and a Safeway store adjacent. Access to bus services (5, 55, 555) at Bridge 127. Visitor Moorings.

Carnforth: *PO; Stores; Tel; Banks; Station.* Carnforth grew from a small village with the coming of first the canal and then the railway. There are frequent bus services from here to the nearby places of interest. Trains leave here for Barrow, Lancaster/Preston; Manchester Airport and the Skipton line.

Pine Lake Resort A mile north of Carnforth on the A6/M6 jcn. Watersports. Tel: 01524 736190.

Warton Village and **Warton Crag** A mile and a half north of Carnforth. A charming village. St. Oswalds Church dates back to the 13th century. The ruins of the old 14th century Manor House can be seen. Strong connections with the 'Washington' family are reflected throughout the village. Warton Crag has an iron age fort at its summit. From here there is a marvellous view of Morecambe Bay.

BOATYARDS
Nu-Way Acorn Carnforth. Slipway, gas, diesel, water and sanitary station Moorings, winter storage. Tel: 01524 734457.

CAMPING AND CARAVANING
Marsh House Farm Camping & Caravan Site, A mile NW of bridge 127 at Crag Bank. SD 483 704. Tel 01524 732879.

Netherbeck Camping & Caravan Site, Half a mile NE of bridge 129. SD 509 710. Tel: 01524 735133.

Capernwray Old Hall Caravan Site, A quarter mile east of bridge 131. SD 533 717. Tel: 01524 733276.

Capernwray House Caravan Site, A mile east of bridge 131. SD 539 718. Tel: 01524 732363.

New England, Capernwray, Canalside, N. of Br. 133. 01524 732612

PUBS
County Hotel, Lancaster Rd, Carnforth. Br. 128, towpath side, 100 m. Meals lunch & evening. Children. Tel: 01524 73249.

Carnforth Hotel, Market St, Carnforth, 128, towpath side, 125 m. Bar meals lunch & evening. Children. Tel: 01524 732902

Royal Station Hotel, Carnforth. Bridge 128, towpath side, 400 m across crossroads. Bar meals lunch & evening. Restaurant. Children. Accommodation, Traditional beers.

Canal Turn, Carnforth, towpath, adjacent filling station. Bar meals lunch & evening, restaurant, children. Tel: 01524 734750.

Cross Keys, Kellet Road, Bridge 128, 100 m. Bar meals lunch & evening. Children. 01524 732749

Eagles Head, Over Kellet, Bridge 130, half mile. Bar meals lunch & evening. Children, garden. 01524 732457

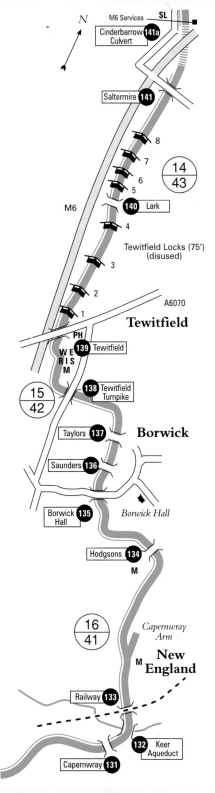

Just north of Capernwray Bridge is the Keer Aqueduct. Like that of the Lune, this was designed by John Rennie. It has a span of 43 feet (13m) and carries the canal 35 feet (11m) above the River Keer. Beyond is Capernwray Canal Arm, known locally as Lover's Creek. This took barges into the heart of Webber Quarry, where they were loaded with limestone. A narrow gauge railway ran around the site, which had quarry workers houses called 'New England'. The remains of the loading cranes can be seen close to the caravan site. As the canal approaches its terminus, it passes Borwick Hall, an Elizabethan manor house built around a defensive Peel tower. Charles II stayed here in 1651 when his army camped in a nearby field. The hall now has a summer café and accommodation. Close to Bridge 138, the last bridge on the cruising length, is Tewitfield picnic site and mooring. A little further is Tewitfield terminus. The canal ended here until 1819 and in 1968, with the building of the M6, it again became the terminus. Tewitfield has visitor moorings, sanitary station, hotel and nearby campsite. North of the terminus on the other side of the road blockage, are the eight disused Tewitfield Locks. North of Saltermire Bridge at Cinderbarrow is the first place where the canal is culverted under the M6.

Tewitfield Locks The 8 locks lift the canal 75 feet over a distance of three-quarters of a mile. They are the only locks on the 57 mile main line and were not opened until the canal was extended to Kendal in 1819, 20 years after the Preston to Tewitfield section was opened. When the express passenger boats arrived at the foot of the locks, the passengers had to disembark, walk up the locks and get into another 'packet' boat waiting at the top of the locks to continue their journey. This enabled the horse drawn boats to maintain their average speed of 10 miles per hour. The locks were officially closed in 1968 when the M6 was constructed, but had been disused for several years.

Continued on next page

Leighton Hall. A mile and a half due west of Tewitfield Locks by public footpath to Yealand Conyers or bus from Carnforth. A Georgian Mansion containing furniture made by R. Gillow of Lancaster, surrounded by attractive grounds and near the coast. It also houses the Birds of Prey Conservation Centre. There are displays of flying eagles daily at 15:30 in fine weather. Open May to September. Tel: 01524 734474.

Leighton Moss 2 miles west of Tewitfield Locks. RSPB nature reserve of reed marshes and large meres. It is the breeding ground of reed warblers and bitterns, but kestrels and shovellers can also be observed from the hides. Access permits can be obtained at seven days notice from the Reserves Dept, The Lodge, Sandy, Beds. or at the Reserve. Tel. 01524 701601.

Silverdale and **Arnside** 3 miles north-west of Carnforth. Area of outstanding natural beauty with many public walks. Details from the Lancaster Tourist Information Office. 01524 32878.

CAMPING AND CARAVANING

Gatelands Camping & Caravan Site, quarter of a mile east of bridge 138 at Tewitfield, SD 521 737 Tel 01524 781133.

PUBS

Longlands Hotel, Canal terminus. Restaurant, Bar meals (lunch & evening). Children for meals only. Accommodation, Function Suite. Tel. 01524 781256.

Borwick Hall, Summer café, accommodation. tel: 01524 732508

THE NORTHERN REACHES
142 – 153

The isolated and un-navigable sections of the canal north of Tewitfield are referred to as the Northern Reaches. The canal is still in water for a further 8 miles to Stainton, acting as a water supply channel from the main feeder which comes from the reservoir at Killington. The channel is generally weed free with an adequate depth of water for canoes or small craft, although portages are necessary round several blockages along the canal. Walkers, however, can still follow the canal all the way to Kendal, which is very worthwhile. The towpath is a public right of way from now on and is excellent where the original canal still exists, and can easily be followed along those stretches that have been infilled. Once away from the noise of the motorway, the canal traverses peaceful countryside, with excellent views of the lakeland fells and a good variety of flora and fauna. A public bus service runs from Kendal to Tewitfield passing through several other villages along the route (Service 555; hourly). 350 m east of Br. 142 Yealand Road, Lancashire County Council have converted a disused refuse tip into a picnic site and car park on which Lancaster & Morecambe model Engineering Society have constructed a miniature railway. For details of running times etc. Tel. 01539 560278.

Small craft can be launched from the slipway at Cinderbarrow Culvert, contact BW 01524 751888. Leaving Cinderbarrow the canal passes through quiet countryside, although one never quite loses the roar from the motorway and the nearby railway occasionally makes its presence known. One soon reaches the old wharf that served the village of Burton-in-Kendal. The canal leaves Lancashire and enters Cumbria and soon the village of Holme. Along here can be seen an example of the stone mileposts that marked the distances between Kendal and Lancaster. North of Holme the canal is culverted under North Road, ending an intact three and a half mile stretch from Cinderbarrow.

Continued on next page

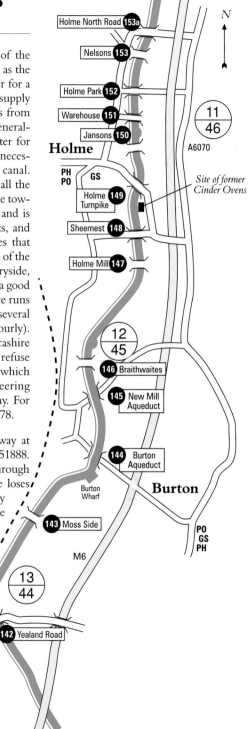

Holme: *PO; Stores; Tel.* An old greystone village. New houses have recently been built along the canal and the owners tend the towpath well along their stretch of canal.

Burton-in-Kendal: *PO; Tel; Stores.* Large interesting village 800 m east of Burton Aqueduct. Useful for shops and 2 pubs.

Heron Corn Mill and Papermaking Museum, two miles west of Holme on the A6 at Beetham. A restored mill dating back to c.1750. Open Tues. – Sun., Easter to Sept.

11am–5pm. Also Bank Holiday Mondays. Tel. 015395 65000.

Lakeland Wildlife Oasis, Wildlife Centre on A6, 1¼ miles west of Burton-in-Kendal. tel 015395 63027.

CROOKLANDS • 154 – 168

North of Holme, the canal is again culverted under the M6. Follow the signposted short diversion across the field alongside the motorway, to rejoin the canal at Dukes Bridge. The canal and everything around is dominated by the 265m high Farleton Fell, which makes an impressive backdrop to this very pleasant stretch of canal. At Farleton there are the remains of a canalside packet house which was once a busy stable and a stopping point for the fast passenger packet boats like 'Swiftsure' and 'Waterwitch'. The canal is again navigable for well over a mile going past Dovehouses Bridge to Moss Side Culvert, where the A65 crosses on an embankment following realignment of the M6. Walkers can use the pedestrian underpass to continue along the canal, now dredged and navigable, for a short distance, until it is again culverted under the M6 embankment, where it crosses the adjacent A65. The motorway leaves the canal at last and there is a further 2½ miles of intact canal as far as Stainton. The main water supply enters just before Crooklands Aqueduct. Up to 17 million gallons of water a day feed into the canal here from Killington Reservoir, 5 miles to the north. The reservoir was completed in 1819 and holds 766 million gallons when full. Motorists get a good view of the reservoir as they stop at Killington Lake Services on the southbound carriageway of the M6 in Cumbria. At Crooklands, the offside wharf is now a coalyard and on the towpath the once-derelict stables now completely restored by the Lancaster Canal Trust, houses a small exhibition featuring the Northern Reaches. The Trust's trip boat *NB Waterwitch* operates from this site, adjacent Bridge 166, during summer weekends and Bank Holidays. There is a picnic site and an explanatory panel about the role of adjacent Wakefield's Wharf, built to serve the local gunpowder factory.

CAMPING END CARAVANING

Millness Hill Holiday Park, Canalside at bridge 163. Self catering chalets, statics and touring park. Tel. 015395 67306.

Little Acre Caravan Park, Crooklands. Canalside by Br. 166. Tourers, electric. Tel. 015395 67214.

Waters Edge Caravan Park, Offside 300m south of Br 166 on A65. Tel. 015395 67708

PUBS

Crooklands Hotel, Canalside by bridge 166. Bar meals lunch & evening. Restaurant lunch & evening. Children. Accommodation. Tel. 015395 67432

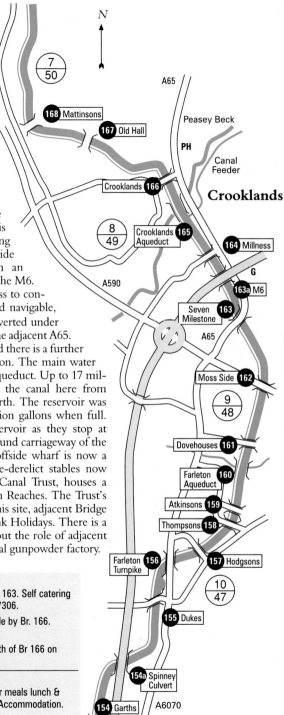

Crooklands

The canal remains in water as far as Stainton Bridge. It provides good fishing, with tench being in abundance. From Stainton northwards, the canal is no longer in water. Just before Hincaster Tunnel, the canal is split by the A590. At the other end of Hincaster Tunnel the canal runs north for 400 m, overlooking the woods of Levens Park and the Kent valley, before it is again cut, and this time disastrously so, by the A590, which passes through a wide sloping cutting well below canal level. The walker must leave the canal before this obstruction is reached and follow the adjacent minor road for 800 m, until it crosses a bridge over the A590. At the north end of the bridge look up the bank for a stile with a footpath sign to Hawes Bridge via towpath. Once over the stile, the walker can be forgiven for thinking that this is not the correct way, because the canal was obliterated in 1985 when the local farmer 'landscaped' the canal into the adjacent fields. However, head NNE, across the field in the direction of the canal bridge in the distance. This used to be a very impressive stretch of canal, cut into the hillside with excellent views. The line of the canal reappears and remains as far as the grand structure of Sedgwick Aqueduct, an ancient monument, which towers above the village. 200 m further on the canal is again obliterated across farmland but can be followed along the line of a hedge on the left for 600 m to a kissing gate in the far left hand corner of the field. It then continues for 600 m through a bridge which now stands isolated in the middle of the next field and serves no purpose except as a shelter for the cattle.

The canal bed reappears and there is a pleasant leafy walk through a cutting to Larkrigg Hall Bridge, where the canal comes into the open. Beyond Crowpark Bridge, the canal has been filled in to the level of the adjacent farmland and will not be seen again for the rest of the way to Kendal, which is now visible in the distance.

Hincaster Tunnel. This is 380 yards long and is the only tunnel on the canal. It was built to take barges close to Sedgwick Gunpowder Works. The tunnel has no towpath so the barges were hauled through by means of a rope fixed on a side wall, or were 'legged' through by the boatmen, by pushing against the tunnel sides with their feet. The horses were led over the tunnel along the horse path which today's walker must follow. This footpath is an interesting feature which has the status of an ancient monument. The tunnel portals are listed buildings. The building at the western portal is a typical stable for the swift packet boat service from Kendal to Preston. Reaching speeds of up to 12 mph between stops the horses were changed every five miles or so; the next stable southbound can be seen adjacent Bridge 155 at Farleton.

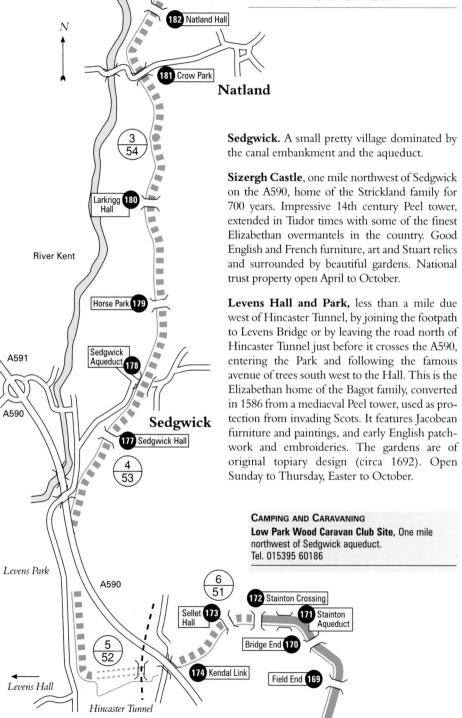

Sedgwick. A small pretty village dominated by the canal embankment and the aqueduct.

Sizergh Castle, one mile northwest of Sedgwick on the A590, home of the Strickland family for 700 years. Impressive 14th century Peel tower, extended in Tudor times with some of the finest Elizabethan overmantels in the country. Good English and French furniture, art and Stuart relics and surrounded by beautiful gardens. National trust property open April to October.

Levens Hall and Park, less than a mile due west of Hincaster Tunnel, by joining the footpath to Levens Bridge or by leaving the road north of Hincaster Tunnel just before it crosses the A590, entering the Park and following the famous avenue of trees south west to the Hall. This is the Elizabethan home of the Bagot family, converted in 1586 from a mediaeval Peel tower, used as protection from invading Scots. It features Jacobean furniture and paintings, and early English patchwork and embroideries. The gardens are of original topiary design (circa 1692). Open Sunday to Thursday, Easter to October.

CAMPING AND CARAVANING
Low Park Wood Caravan Club Site, One mile northwest of Sedgwick aqueduct.
Tel. 015395 60186

53

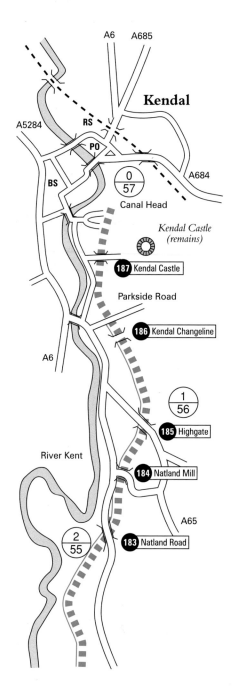

From Natland to Kendal the canal has been filled in but the original line can still be followed even though it is now used as factory yards, car parks or gardens. The line of the towing path is a public right of way all the way to the terminus in Kendal. From Natland Hall Bridge, the canal ran northwards across farmland along the line of a hedge on the left, before crossing Natland Road. It ran alongside the road for a short distance to Natland Mill Bridge, where the line is again evident in a cutting. At Kendal Changeline Bridge, the towpath changed to the east side of the canal. This is the only occurrence of a turnover bridge in Cumbria and is a listed building. The bridge has recently been restored under a Kendal Civic Society initiative. The towpath is now used as a cycleway all the way to the terminus and the canal itself is mainly used as a linear car and lorry park. The last 400 m below Kendal Castle presents a sorry sight and a sad ending to a lovely canal.

The buildings and history of the industry surrounding Canal Head in Kendal are well described in *Kendal's Canal: History, Industry and People'* by John Satchell, published in 2001 by Kendal Civic Society, price £11.95. Many of the buildings associated with the early years of the canal in Kendal have been destroyed or dramatically altered, but there are sufficient buildings left to hint at the importance of the canal, opened in 1819, to the development of Kendal. Several of the existing buildings date from the years of prosperity that followed the canal opening. The original basin has been infilled but some coping stones are visible just inside the Council Depot yard. Canal Head North and Canal Head South define the area of the original basin, and Canal Head Cottage remains as the

CAMPING AND CARAVANING
Millcrest Caravan Site A mile & a half NE of the canal terminus at Millcrest on the A6. SD 525 948. Tel: 01539 21075.

PUBS
There are many pubs and restaurants in the centre of Kendal.

(extended) house of the Canal Agent. Just north of Parkside Road there are some buildings of the Kendal Gas Light and Coke Company that opened in 1825 with coal delivered by canal to its own wharf.

The centre of Kendal is reached by turning left at the terminus and heading west across the River Kent. Buses run from here back to Tewitfield and Carnforth. **Kendal** Charming old stone market town on the River Kent. There are narrow cobbled streets and a mediaeval Shambles. Several attractive 18th century stone bridges span the River Kent. The Gothic Parish Church, which stands alongside the river, is one of the widest in the country. Kendal is also the 'gateway' to the Lake District.

Kendal Castle Little remains of the original Norman castle. Katherine Parr, the last wife of Henry VIII, lived here with her father who was lord of the castle. **Museum of Lakeland Life and Industry** Reconstructed workshops and intimate farmhouse rooms housing local industries and culture. Open Mon–Sat. Tel: 01539 722464. **Abbot Hall Art Gallery** One of Britain's finest small, independent galleries housed in a Georgian house built in 1759, with masterpieces by George Romney, portraits by Daniel Gardner, and watercolours by John Ruskin. Coffee shop. Open Mon–Sat. Tel: 01539 722464. **Kendal Museum** An indoor nature trail of realistic habitats, reconstructed to show the wealth of Lakeland natural history. It also tells the fascinating story of local people from the stone age to the present day. Open Monday to Saturday. Tel: 01539 721374. **Quaker Tapestry** 77 unique panels chronicling Quaker life throughout the centuries. open march – December; Mon–Sat. Tel 01539 722975.

186 Kendal Changeline